# SpringerBriefs in Political Science

SpringerBriefs present concise summaries of cutting-edge research and practical applications across a wide spectrum of fields. Featuring compact volumes of 50 to 125 pages, the series covers a range of content from professional to academic. Typical topics might include:

- A timely report of state-of-the art analytical techniques
- A bridge between new research results, as published in journal articles, and a contextual literature review
- A snapshot of a hot or emerging topic
- An in-depth case study or clinical example
- A presentation of core concepts that students must understand in order to make independent contributions

SpringerBriefs in Political Science showcase emerging theory, empirical research, and practical application in political science, policy studies, political economy, public administration, political philosophy, international relations, and related fields, from a global author community.

SpringerBricfs are characterized by fast, global electronic dissemination, standard publishing contracts, standardized manuscript preparation and formatting guidelines, and expedited production schedules.

Syed Hamid bin Syed Jaafar Albar

# Ibn Khaldun's Theory and the Party-Political Edifice of the United Malays National Organisation

Edited by Mansoureh Ebrahimi

 Springer

Syed Hamid bin Syed Jaafar Albar
Kuala Lumpur, Malaysia

ISSN 2191-5466          ISSN 2191-5474  (electronic)
SpringerBriefs in Political Science
ISBN 978-981-19-7387-1          ISBN 978-981-19-7388-8  (eBook)
https://doi.org/10.1007/978-981-19-7388-8



This Springer imprint is published by the registered company Springer Nature Singapore Pte Ltd.
The registered company address is: 152 Beach Road, #21-01/04 Gateway East, Singapore 189721,
Singapore

# Acknowledgements

All praise is due to Allah (*s.w.t.*), the Creator and Lord of the universe, for giving me the guidance, knowledge and strength to complete this research.

There are many whom I should thank for making this dream a reality. I registered for the Master's Degree programme at the age of 74+ and completed it at 75+. This undertaking would not have been possible without the help and encouragement of others. Among them I would like to specifically mention Prof. Dato' Sri Dr. Ashgar Ali Bin Ali Mohamed, the then Dean of Ahmad Ibrahim Kulliyyah of Laws (AIKOL), International Islamic University Malaysia (IIUM); and my friend, Asst. Prof. Dr. Muhamad Hassan Bin Ahmad of AIKOL, IIUM. They took the trouble to guide me on the process and procedure to undertake the study. I was introduced to Prof. Dr. Mohammad Abdul Quayum Abdus Salam, the then Dean of Kulliyyah of Islamic Revealed Knowledge and Human Sciences (IRKHS), IIUM by Prof. Dato' Sri Dr. Ashgar Ali Bin Ali Mohamed, who made the beginning possible. The rest is all history of how my pursuit of knowledge began.

I would like to express my heartfelt gratitude to Prof. Dato' Sri Dr. Syed Arabi Bin Syed Abdullah Idid, my Supervisor, Prof. Dr. Wahabuddin Ra'ees (Deputy Dean, Postgraduate and Research, IRKHS) and Assoc. Prof. Dr. Hazizan Bin Md. Noon, the co-supervisors for their understanding and patience. My special thanks extend to Prof. Dr. Wahabuddin Ra'ees for his valuable assistance, constant discussions, suggestions, encouragement and meticulous guidance in my research as well as while writing the thesis. Truly, without his tireless effort it would not have been possible for me to complete it. He was kind and generous with his time. I respectfully extend my deepest appreciation to Assoc. Prof. Dr. Mansoureh Ebrahimi for serving as editor of my dissertation, which made this book possible. I would like to express my thanks and regards to senior editor of Social Sciences and Humanities, Ms. Alex Westcott Campbell, and her editorial team at Springer Nature for their invaluable support and assistance. May Allah (*s.w.t.*) reward each and every one of them abundance, success and good health. In undertaking this study, my home environment and encouragement played an important role.

I would like to thank my dear wife, Sharifah Aziah Binti Syed Zainal Abidin; even though she could not understand why I needed to pursue another degree, she was always there with patience and love to assist me. She has been a source of continuous inspiration for me. My children and children-in-law have been wonderful and considerate, and I, therefore, thank them all for their support and encouragement. My special thanks go to my daughter Sharifah Nurzaima Binti Syed Hamid Albar who tirelessly assisted me with the typing and arrangement of the thesis and research though she is busy with her own job; my eldest daughter, Sharifah Thuraya Binti Syed Hamid Albar, and her husband, Haidar, who were accommodating in editing and making suggestions on some aspects of the thesis; Syed Sadiq Bin Syed Hamid Albar for his input on how I could strengthen the thesis; and Ahmad Addan for assisting me in coordinating the safekeeping of my thesis work file. I would also like to acknowledge my gratitude to Rajaa, who was helpful in the editing of two chapters and some others who have helped but whose names I have not mentioned.

Last, but not least, I would like to thank IIUM and its staff for taking me in as a research student and providing me with the necessary facilities.

May Allah (*s.w.t.*) bless all of them and grant success in this life and hereafter.

# Description of the Book

This study examines the decline and erosion of UMNO as a dominant political party of Malaysia through the perspective of Ibn Khaldun's theory of *'asabiyyah* and *'umran*. It uses the qualitative method of data collection from Ibn Khaldun's original works. After discussing Ibn Khaldun's theory of *'asabiyyah* and *'umran*, it looks in detail at UMNO's *'umranic* contributions and erosion of Malay *'asabiyyah*. The research outlines how *'asabiyyah* led UMNO rise to prominence, gain political power and bring progress and development of Malaysia to an *'umranic* stage before it started to decline and erode in concordance with the five stages of Ibn Khaldun's theory of rise and fall of civilisations. This book highlights that early leaders of UMNO played a significant role in fostering group feeling and solidarity among the Malays (*'asabiyyah*). *'Asabiyyah* was the engine that propelled UMNO to acquire *mulk* and transform the Malays and Malaysia to an *'umranic* society. In conclusion, the later leaders of UMNO contributed to weakening of the Malay *'asabiyyah* and the fall of UMNO from power in the 14th General Election in 2018. The process of UMNO's decline and erosion of the political power has been primarily caused by the leaders' failures and shortcomings. The study, among others, recommends that for UMNO to be relevant again in the current political landscape, it must initiate new and serious approaches and initiatives to change itself and must focus on good governance and rule of law in a multi-ethnic Malaysian society.

This book provides a comprehensive review of the social transformation brought about by *'umran*, includes in-depth discussions on the loosening of solidarity or *'asabiyyah* within the Malay Muslim society, covers a vast array of the operationalisation of Ibn Khaldun's theory, illustrating the many factors that led to the decline of political power and dominance of UMNO. It adds value to the corpus of knowledge and seeks to fill the gap on the applicability of Ibn Khaldun's political theory to the UMNO dilemma. This book covers a vast array of the operationalisation of Ibn Khaldun's theory of *'asabiyyah* and *'umran* to the decline of political power and dominance of UMNO and its leadership of Malaysia from GE12 in 2008 until GE14 in 2018. Finally, it examines whether Ibn Khaldun's theory of *'asabiyyah* and *'umran* would be relevant to UMNO today and discusses how it could be applied by illustrating the numerous factors responsible for the decline of UMNO. The findings of the study offer suggestions if UMNO wants to regain power and rise again.

# Contents

# About the Author

**Tan Sri Dr. "Syed Hamid bin Syed Jaafar Albar" Chairman World Islamic Economic Forum Foundation**

Tan Sri Dr. Syed Hamid began his career in the Judicial and Legal Service as a magistrate in 1970 and was appointed the President of the Sessions Court in 1971. He then pursued a career in the financial and banking sector locally and internationally from 1972 to 1986. In the years 1986 to 1990, he became a partner in the law firm of Albar, Zulkifly and Yap. He was a Member of Parliament from 1990 to 2013, during which time he held various ministerial positions including Minister in the Prime Minister's Department and Minister of Justice, Minister of Defence, Minister of Home Affairs and most notably, Minister of Foreign Affairs. Tan Sri Dr. Syed Hamid's last held position was Chairman of the Land Public Transport Commission of Malaysia (SPAD), from 2010 to 2017. Tan Sri Dr. Syed Hamid holds a Barrister-at-Law degree from the Middle Temple, U.K. and was called to the Malaysian Bar in 1974. He also holds a Master's Degree in Human Sciences (Political Science) from International Islamic University, Malaysia and a Ph.D. in International Relations from Asia e University, Kuala Lumpur. Tan Sri Dr. Syed Hamid is currently Adjunct Professor of three universities, namely, University Kebangsaan Malaysia (UKM), University Malaya (UM), University Melaka (UNIMEL) and Kuala Lumpur Metropolitan University College (KLMUC) as well as Chairman of the OIC Study Group (OICSG).

Syed Hamid has contributed books, essays and articles to national, regional, international media and academic journals. He appeared in many political and current affairs programmes on BBC, CNN, ALJAZEERA as well as with local TV channels.

He is also actively involved with regional and global humanitarian activities. He was the founder and President of HUMANITI Malaysia, an NGO involved in humanitarian activities. He also served as Special Envoy to Myanmar, of the Organisation of Islamic Cooperation (OIC).

In recognition of his services to the nation, Tan Sri Dr. Syed Hamid was conferred the Order of the Defender of the Realm (PMN) by the King of Malaysia which carries the title "Tan Sri", in 2009. He was conferred the Grand Cordon of the Order of the Rising Sun by The Emperor of Japan in 2019 for his valuable contribution to the development of Malaysia/Japan High Speed Railway and the good relation between Malaysia and Japan.

He is Advocate and Solicitor and Managing Partner in Noor Amran & Co since July 2020.

# Abbreviations

| | |
|---|---|
| 1MDB | One Malaysian Development Berhad |
| Amanah | *Malaysian Parti Amanah Negara* or the National Trust Party |
| BA | Barisan Alternatif or Barisan Alternative or Alternative Front |
| Bersatu | *Parti Pribumi Bersatu Malaysia* or Malaysian United Indigenous Party |
| BN | *Barisan Nasional* or National Front |
| DAP | Democratic Action Party |
| DPM | Deputy Prime Minister |
| FELDA | Federal Land Development Authority |
| GE | General Election |
| GERAKAN | Malaysian People's Movement Party |
| GST | Goods and Sales Tax |
| HINDRAF | Hindu Rights Action Force |
| IIUM | International Islamic University Malaysia |
| IMP | Independent Malayan Party |
| ITM | Institut Teknologi MARA |
| MCA | Malaysian Chinese Association |
| MIC | Malaysia Indian Congress |
| MPAJA | Malayan People's Anti-Japanese Army |
| MRSM | *Maktab Rendah Sains MARA* or Junior Science College MARA |
| MU | Malayan Union Constitution |
| NEP | New Economic Policy |
| NOC | National Operations Council |
| PAP | People Action Party of Singapore |
| PMIP | Pan Malayan Islamic Party |
| PAS | *Parti Islam Se-Malaysia* or Malaysian Islamic Party |
| PBUH | Peace Be Upon Him |
| PERKEMBAR | *Pertubuhan Kebangsaan Melayu Bersatu* |
| PH | *Pakatan Harapan* |
| PKN | *Parti Keadilan Nasional* or National Justice Party |
| PKR | *Parti Keadilan Rakyat* or People's Justice Party |

| | |
|---|---|
| PM | Prime Minister |
| PMSJ | *Pergerakan Melayu Semenanjung Johor* or Peninsular Malay Movement of Johore |
| PNM | *Parti Negara Malaya* |
| PR | *Pakatan Rakyat* or People's Alliance |
| SRC | SRC International |
| UDA | Urban Development Authority |
| UiTM | Universiti Teknologi MARA |
| UKM | Universiti Kebangsaan Malaysia |
| UMNO | United Malays National Organisation |
| USM | Universiti Sains Malaysia |
| WWII | World War II |

# Chapter 1
# UMNO: A Malay Ethnic-Based Political Party

**Abstract** This chapter discusses the statement of the problem, significance of the study, gap in existing literature, theoretical framework of the study and the research design and method of data collection. The United Malays National Organisation (UMNO), a Malay ethnic-based political party was founded on 11 May 1946, and has been the dominant driving force in the politics of Malaya under Parti Perikatan (Alliance Party) from independence in 1957 until 1974. After the formation of Malaysia on 16 September 1963, it continued to govern the country within the framework of National Front or Barisan Nasional (BN) until it lost power on 8 May 2018. UMNO from the time of its establishment struggled to champion the rights of the ethnic Malays through several policy initiatives such as the New Economic Policy (NEP), sustaining the constitutional rights and privileges of the Malays within the context of the 'social contract'.

**Keywords** Malaya · The British · *Malayan Union* · UMNO · *Parti Perikatan* · *Barisan Nasional* · Ibn Khaldun's Theory

## 1.1  Introduction

The United Malays National Organisation (UMNO), a Malay ethnic-based political party, was founded on 11 May 1946. UMNO has been the dominant driving force in the politics of Malaya under *Parti Perikatan* (Alliance Party) since the independence of Malaya in 1957 until 1974. After the formation of Malaysia on 16 September 1963, UMNO continued to govern the country within the framework of National Front or *Barisan Nasional* (BN) until it lost power on 8 May 2018. UMNO, from the time of its establishment, has championed the rights of the ethnic Malays through several policy initiatives such as the New Economic Policy (NEP), sustaining the constitutional rights and privileges of the Malays within the context of the 'social contract'. The government has been largely successful in transforming the rural-based Malay community into a modern civic ethnic community. UMNO was the only political party at the time of the struggle for independence acceptable to the


S. H. bin Syed Jaafar Albar, *Ibn Khaldun's Theory and the Party-Political Edifice of the United Malays National Organisation*, SpringerBriefs in Political Science,
https://doi.org/10.1007/978-981-19-7388-8_1

British, the Malay Rulers, the aristocrats and the Malay masses. Other Malay ethnic-based political parties such as *Parti Pribumi Bersatu* Malaysia or Malaysian United Indigenous Party (Bersatu), *Parti Islam Se-Malaysia* or Malaysian Islamic Party (PAS) and *Parti Keadilan Rakyat* or People's Justice Party (PKR) are in fact the offshoots of UMNO except for the Malaysian *Parti Amanah Negara* or the National Trust Party (Amanah), which was the offshoot of PAS. UMNO's leadership has been able to garner the support of other major ethnic groups through the politics of coalition and compromise. UMNO, while championing the rights of the Malay ethnic community, adopted a policy of moderation towards other races. Therefore, it has been instrumental in delivering economic development to Malaysia and maintaining peace and racial harmony. UMNO enjoyed strong popularity among the Malays until the 10th General Election (GE) in 1999.

But, in the 9 May 2018 GE, UMNO's 61-year rule abruptly came to an end. The regime change in that election through the democratic ballot box in Malaysia was radical and phenomenal and should, hence, be critically examined by analysing the general election results between 2008 and 2018. This will allow us to comprehend the factors contributing to the rise and decline of the political power of UMNO as a driving political force in Malaysian politics. For this purpose, the researcher will apply the political theories of fourteenth-century Muslim philosopher and historian Ibn Khaldun's theory of *'umran* (science of civilisation/culture) and *'asabiyyah* (social solidarity/group feeling). It was clear that support for UMNO among Malay voters declined due to the issues of governance and corruption, and financial scandals coupled with the disintegration of group feeling and/or solidarity (i.e., *'asabiyyah*). Viewing it from the perspective of Ibn Khaldun's theory of *'asabiyyah*, one could suggest alternative ways of reinstating group feeling for UMNO members and a sense of confidence to regain their solidarity and cohesion and restore the people's (*rakyat's*) confidence in the party leadership. The Malay community, who are Muslims, faces many challenges and problems at the state and national levels. The Malays need strong and credible party leaders to lead them under UMNO to prevent a further decline in their power and regain their popularity and strength. Therefore, there are many examples and lessons from Ibn Khaldun's theory of *'asabiyyah* and *'umran* that can be applied to arrest the downhill slide of the political power of UMNO since the 2008 GE up until its removal from power in 2018.

## 1.2   UMNO Response to the British Colony

The formation of UMNO was a strong reaction to the British scheme to make Malaya and the Straits Settlement a British colony after World War II (WWII). They were certain that the Malays would never rise or be united. On the contrary, the divide and rule policy, and importing migrant ethnic groups as workers, would, in the British view, minimise the possible rise of political consciousness in the Malay States. On top of that, the British inculcated 'state consciousness or loyalty to the state' (*semangat kenegerian*) so that the Malays would not be united as one national group. Thus, the introduction of the Malayan Union Constitution (MU) was a perfect solution to give them absolute power over Malaya. At the same time, the British sought solutions on how to overcome problems associated with the two million migrants they brought into the country on a temporary basis. Cleverly, under duress, the British managed to get all the Sultans to sign an agreement on the proposed colonial arrangement. Abdullah Zakaria Ghazali (2012: 15) (see original text in Bahasa Malaysia in footnote)[1] said: "In 1946 the British government decided to introduce the MU in the Federation of Malaya after Sir Harold MacMichael obtained the signatures of all the Malay Rulers consenting to it". Hence, the colonial government did not expect any opposition from the Malay population. However, they underestimated the reaction of the Malays. As Abdullah said: "The introduction of the MU provoked opposition from the Malay population. They were dissatisfied with the granting of citizenship to the foreigners (non-Malays) on very flexible terms, the loss of power of the Malay Rulers, who were left with the responsibility of controlling matters of Malay customs and Islamic religion only" (Ghazali 2012: 15) (see original text in Bahasa Malaysia in the footnote).[2]

The British had totally misread the Malay feelings on the issues of citizenship, and the position of the Malay Rulers and how they interpreted the British action to the question of sovereignty of the country and status of the Malay rulers. The Malays revolted against the British because they considered it as an affront to their dignity and sovereignty. The narrative of this feeling is encapsulated in the Malay saying and slogan '*Mendaulatkan Martabat Bangsa*' (giving sovereignty to the dignity of the Malays). The Malays can be passive, tolerant and considerate but not when it affects their honour and dignity. The Malay ethos was clearly expressed as "the customs of being kith and kin, their position must be defended; the tradition of living in the same village, the village must be protected; the prerequisite of being of the same race, unity must be given priority" (see original text in Bahasa Malaysia in footnote)[3] (Jaafar, 1946, as cited in UMNO Johor, n.d.).

This was the battle cry for unity and acted as a common cause for defending the dignity and sovereignty of the country. UMNO was formed when the British interfered with this dignity and sovereignty of the Malays as a race and original people of the land. The introduction of MU had the reverse affect as it engendered group feelings. In this regard, it can be said the Malay battle cry can be associated with an imagined community moving together to reinstate its dignity and sovereignty. The introduction of MU, according to the write up on "*Sejarah Penubuhan UMNO*", was contrary to what was agreed to by the British to sustain a pro-Malay policy consistent with the recognition that Malaya was a Malay country. As stated in the

---

[1] "*Kemudiannya pada tahun 1946 kerajaan British memperkenalkan Malayan Union di Tanah Melayu, setelah Sir Harold MacMichael mendapat tandatangan daripada semua Raja-Raja Melayu*".

[2] "*Pengenalan Malayan Union ini mencetuskan tentangan daripada orang Melayu. Mereka tidak puas hati terhadap kerakyatan yang longgar diberikan kepada orang asing, dan kehilangan kuasa raja Melayu, yang hanya berkuasa dalam adat dan agama Islam sahaja*".

[3] "*Adat bersaudara, saudara di pertahankan; adat berkampung kampung di jaga; adat berbangsa, perpaduan bangsa di utamakan*".

same article: "The pro-Malay policy before the Second World War is going to be abandoned contemporaneously, and the Malays as the indigenous people will have to compete at par with the migrant races" (see original text in Bahasa Malaysia in footnote)[4] (UMNO Information, n.d.). The MU, therefore, was seen as intending to change the *status quo*.

Wan Hashim Wan Teh (2017) in his article "*Fasa pertama perjuangan UMNO penuh berani*" (the First Phase of UMNO's Struggle with Courage) says during the first phase of UMNO's struggle from 1946 to 1951 under the leadership of Dato' Onn Jaafar, the unity of the Malays was strong when different organisations at the state and district levels were vocal and courageous in opposing the MU. He writes: "With unity and solidarity of the Malays, the associations and organisations at the state and district levels decided to merge, even before UMNO was officially formed as a political party, forcefully and courageously voicing their opposition to the MU scheme that the British government wanted to introduce upon returning after the war to make Malaya a full-fledged colony of Britain from just being protectorates" (see original text in Bahasa Malaysia in the footnote).[5]

The MU scheme brought about nationalism and unity of the Malays. The Malays set aside their individual positions and came together to fight against the unjust action of the British. The Malay associations, organisations and movements of divergent philosophies and ideologies throughout Malaya held The Malay Congress of Malaya (*Kongres Melayu Se Malaya*) from 1 to 4 March 1946, and 41 Malay organisations who attended the meeting agreed to merge and dissolve themselves to form one political party under one body called UMNO for the sake of survival of the Malays. With this, they possessed a common platform and shared values. It was the British act, done without consultation, that had changed them "from having a very diverse and narrow state sentiment and viewpoints, they saw the reality confronting them, and rose to oppose such scheme" (see original text in Bahasa Malaysia in the footnote)[6] (Wan Teh 2017). They rose spontaneously and became united for a common cause to protect their position and status in their own country. Under the leadership of Dato' Onn Jaafar, the party was formed on 11 May 1946. Their main struggle was to oppose the British scheme to overwhelm their race through migrants politically and economically.

The Third Malay Congress in 1946 held at the Sultan Sulaiman Club, Kampung Baru Kuala Lumpur was the Malay reaction to MU. It was at this Congress that

---

[4] "*Dasar pro Melayu sebelum perang akan di rombak sekaligus, dan orang Melayu sebagai penduduk asal negara ini terpaksa bersaing dengan orang-orang mendatang*".

[5] "*Dengan kesatuan yang kukuh dalam kalangan orang Melayu yang bergabung melalui pertubuhan masing-masing di peringkat negeri dan daerah, orang Melayu ketika UMNO belum lagi lahir secara rasmi sebagai sebuah pertubuhan politik, bersuara lantang dengan penuh keberanian menentang gagasan Malayan Union yang cuba di perkenal oleh Inggeris yang datang semula untuk menjadikan Semenanjung Tanah Melayu sebagai tanah jajahannya dengan secara mutlak*".

[6] "*Berbagai sentimen kenegeriaan dan pemandangan yang sempit, sekarang mereka melihat realiti di depan mereka, telah bangkit menentang rancangan itu*".

the following decisions and resolutions were made and passed (see original text in Bahasa Malaysia in footnote)[7] (Wan Teh 2017).

1. The Malayan Union Constitution is rejected and is considered unlawful because it did not obtain opinion and consent, through consultation, with the Malay people, who are as the indigenous and legitimate citizens of the Malay States.
2. The Malayan Union Constitution has given the Malays, who are subjects of the Malay Rulers, the same status as that of the ethnic Chinese and Indians, who are not even citizens as yet and who came as temporary migrants or British subjects of the Straits Settlements of Singapore, Malacca and Penang.
3. The Malayan Union Constitution reduced the dignity and sovereignty of the Malay Rulers to just being the Head of Religion and Malay Customs of their individual states. The absolute sovereignty to govern is given to the Governor at the State level and Governor-General at the Federation level.

This Congress was the expression of an uprising or revolt of the Malays towards the British and they called upon the latter to withdraw the MU Constitution. This was successful and the MU Constitution was replaced with the Federation of Malaya Agreement in 1948. UMNO was formed on 11 May 1946 and launched at the Istana Balai Besar, Johor Bharu. This can be likened to a quiet revolution that took over power from the British; finally, Malaya became independent on 31 August 1957 (Wan Teh 2017).

UMNO, after its formation, negotiated for independence for Malaya, which was acceptable to the British, the Malay Rulers and the Malays represented by their aristocrats. With unity and social solidarity of the Malays and the cooperation of the non-Malays through a power sharing formula with the granting of citizenship, the Alliance won political power to govern Malaya from 1957 and, subsequently, Malaysia (from 1974 under the name of BN). They stewarded the country for 61 years without interruption, although at times they went through rough patches. All ethnic communities acquiesced for UMNO helming the leadership of the nation because it was willing to share political power with the non-Malays. The politics of compromise and accommodation has always been UMNO's approach up to today. The country

---

[7] *"Kongres Melayu Se Malaya membuat beberapa ketetapan seperti berikut:*

1. *Perlembagaan Malayan Union itu ditolak dan di anggap tidak sah kerana tidak pernah memperoleh pendapat dan restu, secara berunding dengan rakyat bangsa Melayu sebagai pribumi dan rakyat yang sah bagi negeri-negeri Melayu.*

2. *Perlembagaan Malayan Union meletakkan kedudukan orang Melayu sebagai rakyat baginda Sultan sama taraf dengan kaum Cina dan India yang belum lagi bertaraf warganegara dan hanya sebagai pendatang sementara atau warga Inggeris bagi mereka di negeri-negeri Selat iaitu Singapura, Melaka dan Pulau Pinang.*

3. *Perlembagaan Malayan Union menurunkan martabat Raja-Raja Melayu yang akan bertaraf sebagai Ketua Agama dan Adat Resam Melayu di negeri masing-masing. Kuasa pemerintah sepenuhnya Gabenor diperingkat negeri dan Gabenor Jeneral di peringkat persekutuan".*

became a model developing country in a multi-ethnic, multi-religious and multi-cultural environment. No one can dispute that this achievement came about due to UMNO's ability to bring unity, solidarity of its people and economic development.

This book will analyse and examine the chronology of events and factors that led to the decline of UMNO with specific focus on the GE results from 2008 to 2018. By reviewing the literature on the subject, it is clear that a study on the eroding power of UMNO by applying Ibn Khaldun's political theory of *'asabiyyah* and *'umran* does not exist prior to this research.

## 1.3   Issues That Paved the Way for Downfall

The 61-year rule of UMNO came to an end on 9 May 2018. Many questions have been raised about the nature and causes of the decline of political power of UMNO in Malaysia after GE14 on 9 May 2018. Malay voters' political support for UMNO had eroded and their feeling of being part of the imagined community had disappeared due to the transformation of Malay society from a rural-based society to an urban-based one. Living in a highly urbanised and developed state with sprawling towns and cities had caused changes in their social and traditional values. Therefore, UMNO today faces challenges from within the party as well as challenges emanating from Malaysia's socio-political fabric. The challenges UMNO faces from within are issues of weak leadership(s), such as moral degradation, money politics, corruption, over-centralisation of party matters at the headquarters in Kuala Lumpur, conflicts and disunity. Additionally, its weak leadership of the government, whether perceived or real. There were also issues of coalition partners in the BN. Since GE10, the social media became a significant instrument in forming public opinion on leaders and government. On top of that, the state has achieved an *'umrani* status from urbanisation, which has led to changes in social and traditional values. These internal and external issues resulted in the loss of trust and confidence in the BN government led by UMNO among Malay urban and young voters as well as non-Malay voters. There was a serious credibility and confidence gap in the Malay leadership in a new urbanised environment, which decapitated voters' (Malays and non-Malays) support since within BN itself group feelings and cohesion had weakened, i.e., sense of *'asabiyyah'* towards UMNO as the leader of the BN had disappeared with it. Hence, there is a need to explore, examine and redefine the applicability of the concept of *'asabiyyah* expounded by Ibn Khaldun. With this rationale, it is inevitable that extensive expository research needs to be conducted to explain the determinants, nature and causes of the decline of UMNO based on current realities and new paradigms in the political landscape prevailing in Malaysia today. What measures can be taken to correct the erosion of political powers and dominance of UMNO? This study answers the following questions:

1. How was UMNO's political dominance weakened?
2. What are the factors behind the decline and erosion of the political power and dominance of UMNO?
3. Can Ibn Khaldun's theory of *'asabiyyah* and *'umran* explain the decline of UMNO's political power and dominance in Malaysia and how can it be overcome?

The objectives of this study are:

1. To analyse how UMNO's political power and dominance has weakened over the period 2008–2018.
2. To discuss the causes of the decline of support among the Malays and erosion of UMNO's political power.
3. To discuss Ibn Khaldun's theory *'asabiyyah* and *'umran* and their application to UMNO's decline of political power, and how to overcome this decline.


## 1.4  Causes of UMNO's Decline

Much of the writing concerning Malaysian politics has touched on the declining role of UMNO and focused on the factors behind it. Bridget Welsh (2018) highlights a piece on the decline of UMNO. Contributors to Welsh's work are mainly Malaysian academics and political activists. These writings collectively warned of the crisis within UMNO due to corruption and mismanagement of power and authority. The authors spoke of UMNO misdeeds and the Malay political dynamics that began to push UMNO adrift and led to its rejection by the *rakyat* (citizens). These works also presented a comparative study of UMNO of 1957 and UMNO of 2016 and concluded that the latter had lost credibility and trust of the Malays. They argue that UMNO can regain its legitimacy if it regains its 1957 spirit and sagacity. The authors claim that the UMNO's declining legitimacy in the eyes of the Malays encouraged even the non-Malays to raise their dissatisfaction about this Malay-dominant institution and the UMNO-led state institutions. Welsh (2018) says that what moved UMNO away from its grassroots foundation was that it became "a more elitist, centralised and inward-looking institution without the same level of connectivity with Malaysian society" and the Malay ethnic community. She argues that the UMNO's recent leadership(s) and their inability to reform UMNO were the main causes of the decline of this fallen hero (Welsh 2018: 214–215).

M. Moniruzzaman and K. F. Farzana (2018) argue that the decline of UMNO and the erosion of the Malay dominance began in 1999 when the spat between Tun Dr. Mahathir Mohamad and his then DPM and successor-designate Anwar Ibrahim came into the open. This was the time when he sacked Anwar Ibrahim. According to the authors, in 1999, the Malays became permanently divided and UMNO gave birth to yet another Malay-dominated multi-ethnic political party, PKR. This, according to the writers, challenged the dominance of UMNO. They did not discuss other factors that caused or influenced the decline of UMNO. Scott Edwards (2018) seemingly follows the same line of argument as Moniruzzaman and Farzana (2018) that the erosion of UMNO's legitimacy had started some two decades ago. However, according to Edwards (2018), the factors that contributed to declining legitimacy of UMNO's political power and dominance were people's awareness of the extent of the corruption scandals of Najib Razak involving the One Malaysian Development Berhad (1MDB) and SRC International (SRC). He says five factors were fundamental in raising the awareness of the public. These were: "the scale of corruption; the scale of personal enrichment on the behalf of political leaders; a stagnation in quality of living and unpopular economic policies; the international dimension and the potential role of foreign money; and the role of social media in propagating these issues" (Edwards 2018: 2).

UMNO was one of the longest surviving dominant parties in the world ruling Malaya/Malaysia until GE14 when it was brought down by a new coalition known as *Pakatan Harapan* (PH). Many political writers and observers within and outside the country have described UMNO's defeat in GE14 as a political tsunami or earthquake. This could be more appropriately described as a Malaysian Tsunami (Jason Wei et al. 2021), because the wave was brought about by discontented voters cutting across ethnic lines. Can the fall of UMNO be described as a tsunami or an earthquake? After all it had been in power for the last 61 years and had brought dignity to the Malays, restored the position of the Malay Rulers, and accommodated and compromised with other ethnic groups to achieve independence. UMNO took on the leadership role from the beginning to bring about solidarity and unity of all races in Malaya. The government of the Alliance Party and, after the formation of Malaysia in 1963, the government under BN transformed the country from an agro-based economy to an industrial one, or from rural to sedentary. This book intends to examine what went wrong for a party with a sterling success record to become a party out of power.

## 1.5  Relevance of Ibn Khaldun's Theory of *'asabiyyah* and *'umran* to UMNO in Literature

There are many studies which focus on Ibn Khaldun's biography, theory of state, *'umran* or civilisation/culture, *'asabiyyah* (group feeling), education, law, personality development and spirituality. There are also studies that attempt to apply Ibn Khaldun's theory to specific events and happenings. Though scarce and slowly emerging, there are other studies that discuss the decline and erosion of UMNO's political power. However, there is no study, as will become clear through the following discussion, that explains the decline and erosion of the political power of UMNO through Ibn Khaldun's theory of *'asabiyyah* and *'umran*. Ibn Khaldun crystallised his experiences and observations into concepts and theories, and *'asabiyyah* and *'umran* were borne out of this analysis. Ibn Khaldun's *Muqaddimah* (*Prolegomena* in English) was an introduction to his *"Kitab al- 'Ibar"*, "the Book of Lessons". It has attracted a lot of discussion and debate among scholars and commentators searching for relevancy, significance and comparative analysis to relate it to the notion of social or political change not only during his period but also in the present time (scholars like Caksu [2007], Syed Farid Alatas [2013], M. Akif Kayapinar [2008] have discussed on this subject).

Franz Rosenthal, the first scholar to translate the entire *Muqaddimah* into English (Ibn Khaldun 1958), interprets *'asabiyyah* as 'group feeling'. Some academics like Hodgson (2009) and Garrison (2012) regarded Franz Rosenthal's translation as vague and unsatisfactory. Another scholar Ernest Gellner (1982) interprets *'asabiyyah* by linking it to Durkheim's (1997) theory of organic and mechanical solidarities and Allen Fromherz (2011) takes the same view as Durkheim's concept of solidarity, by translating it to 'tribal solidarity'.

In addition, many, both at theoretical and practical levels, have studied Ibn Khaldun's dynamic study of history. Muhsin Mahdi (1957) eloquently discusses Ibn Khaldun's theory of *'asabiyyah* and *'umran* and argues that for Ibn Khaldun, *'asabiyyah* was instrumental in the development and rise and fall of *'umran*. It is interesting to note that Mahdi argues that in Ibn Khandun's theory of *'umran*, political power and state institutions were central. Yet, power and state were heavily dependent on the result and role of *'asabiyyah*. However, Wahabuddin Ra'ees (2004) argues that in Ibn Khaldun's thought, the state in pursuit of its purposes of justice, equality, order and equity must put some safeguards to protect *'asabiyyah* from drifting into decadence. In Ibn Khaldun's view, *'asabiyyah* should always be placed under the purview of the religion of Islam.

Ra'ees (2013) argues that Ibn Khaldun's theory of state is dynamic and its application viable to all situations, universal and specific. He applies Ibn Khaldun's theory of state to explain the shift in the strategy of the ruling political parties in Egypt, Tunisia and Turkey. Robert Irwin (2018) discusses the intellectual biography of Ibn Khaldun, focusing on turbulent socio-political conditions of the fourteenth-century Muslims in Spain and North Africa that gave rise to Ibn Khaldun's political thought and his analysis of politics of the Muslim state and society. For Irwin, Ibn Khaldun was the most misunderstood scholar of the Muslim world. Allen James Fromherz (2011) joins Irwin in discussing the politics and social conditions in which Ibn Khaldun lived. Fromherz argues that Ibn Khaldun was a very strong critique of blind trust in the tradition that challenged innovation and creativity. In fact, it was this blind imitation of tradition that contributed among others to the decline and decadence of Islamic culture and civilisation. Fromherz explains that even though Ibn Khaldun was a strong opponent of blind trust in tradition, he would subject every human activity to the approval of Prophetic traditions, leaving not much room for individual free will. Many did not agree with Fromherz's view (such as F. Rosenthal, Syed Farid Alatas).

Yumna Ozer (2017) translates Ibn Khaldun's response to the heated debate of his time about the role of the Sufi orders in the development of personality. Ibn Khaldun found it necessary to engage in the discussion of necessity of the teachings of Sufi masters. Ahmad Zaid (2003) provides an interesting discussion on Ibn

Khaldun's source of writing of history and his classification of knowledge into religious and rational sciences. Zaid's discussion on the subject explains Ibn Khaldun's writings on the relationship between revealed knowledge and acquired knowledge. Zaid also discusses the role of Arabic Language and Literature in scholarly writings concerned with development of human institutions. Azmeh (2003) re-reads Ibn Khaldun and argues that he has provided systematic and scientific explanation to the medieval North African and Medieval and modern Arab-Islamic culture and traditions. Azmeh argues that Ibn Khaldun was ahead of his time. According to him, his theoretical and philosophical underpinnings of Muslim socio-political culture have universal application and validity. However, none of the above arguments applies to Ibn Khaldun's theory to political developments, and specifically to the discussion on the eroding power of UMNO.

## 1.6  Theoretical Framework According to Ibn Khaldun's Theory of *'asabiyyah* and *'umran*

This study attempts to confine the framework to *'asabiyyah* and *'umran* as contained in the *Muqaddimah* as the independent variable and decline of UMNO and erosion of its power as a dominant political party as the dependent variable. Ibn Khaldun's concepts of *'asabiyyah* and *'umran* answer the research questions on how society and state are transformed from rural to urban and subsequently its rise and decline. For Ibn Khaldun, *'asabiyyah* and *'umran* are interconnected with each other; one acts as the moving force behind all collective efforts in the political objective for power and dominance before it proceeds to build for growth and development of the state or dynasty. During the period 2008–2018, it has been acknowledged that UMNO's political cohesiveness weakened due to leadership and governance crises. This trend might lead to the total emasculation of UMNO as a political force due to its failure to maintain group feeling and, thus, solidarity within UMNO and the Malay society. Thus, the UMNO leadership should have paid attention to the cause and effect of the erosion. It is discernibly demonstrated that the new coalition that won the 2018 GE has stronger *'asabiyyah* and leadership credibility. The political theory of *'asabiyyah* and *'umran* as contained in the *Muqaddimah* is relevant and of significant value to answer the political and social problems and challenges facing UMNO.

Rosenthal (Ibn Khaldun 1958) when translating the *Muqaddimah* considers the term *'asabiyyah* too vague to be directly translated, but he translated it as 'group feeling'. Even though there were scholars such as Gellner (1982) and Durkheim (1997) who considered the translation as unsatisfactory, the fact remains that he was the first scholar to translate the entire *Muqaddimah* into English. Hodgson (2009) considers Rosenthal's definition deficient. According to Garrison (2012), the phrase group feeling did not reflect the essence of the concept's socio-political characteristics, hence it did not have the strength as a doctrine for social change. Gellner

(1982) brands *'asabiyyah* as social solidarity, though unsatisfactory, it reflected a greater sense of group unity in thought and action. Allen J. Fromherz (2011) borrows the term from Durkheim's (1997) concepts of mechanical solidarity that minimised the translation of *'asabiyyah* to 'tribal solidarity'. Akbar S. Ahmed (2002: 20–45) translates it as 'social cohesion'.

Of course, it could not be said that all these translations encapsulated the multi-dimensional meanings of *'asabiyyah* as envisaged by Ibn Khaldun. This clearly demonstrates that the English translation by the scholars was not able to entirely capture the true historical and contextual meanings of *'asabiyyah.* Under the circumstances, Arslan (1987) says it is better to understand the functions in order to get to the real meaning of the word used. He, thus, agreed that Ibn Khaldun's term be left in its original Arabic term. In his interpretation of the *Muqaddimah*, Mahdi (1957) states one must start from correct information to understand the causes and nature of historical events, but in order to be able to rectify information about events and distinguish the correct facts from fictions, one must know their nature and causes. Lenn Evan Goodman (1972) considers that Khaldun's approach illustrated his demand for clarity, realism and critical thinking.

Mahdi (1957) in *"Ibn Khaldun's Philosophy of History"* interprets *'asabiyyah* as purely social solidarity practised in primitive cultures to explain the nature and characteristics of the state in primitive cultures. He argues that social solidarity originated from natural desire to be compassionate to help and defend one's immediate relations. *'Asabiyyah* as a means to achieve solidarity was a social construct, out of necessity for cooperation and self-defence. Although Mahdi's book was focused on the philosophy of history, it expounds the new science of culture developed by Ibn Khaldun. *'Asabiyyah,* is therefore, the substrate or a social phenomenon for political change and it serves to achieve that objective. However, in order to determine whether the concepts have relevance or practicality in contemporary politics and social change, the researcher first deals with the definition and translation by modern scholars.

The usage of the word *'asabiyyah* in its original Arabic is conceded for various reasons, *inter alia*, many were of the opinion that translation into English would not be easy, rather complex and might not reflect Ibn Khaldun's intended meaning. In the researcher's opinion, even though there was no single or common meaning of the term among scholars, the underlying factors in the translations conveyed the same sense like group feeling, social cohesion, tribal solidarity and social solidarity.

The word *'asabiyyah* had its beginning from the pre-Islamic usage in tribal societies, where it was used to indicate solidarity or group feeling to signify unity in "thought and action, and social and economic cohesiveness among members of the same tribe" (Garrison 2012: 35). The word *'asabiyyah* comes from the Arabic root word, originally meaning "spirit of kinship" (the *'asaba* are male relations in the male line) *'asaba'*, means "kin" or "blood relation", in the family or tribe. According to Rosenthal (1958), Ibn Khaldun used the term because the word was related to the Qur'anic words of *'isaba* and *'usba*, both meaning "group" in the general sense. In the *Hadith*, Prophet Mohammad (PBUH) condemned *'asabiyyah* based purely on loyalty and without consideration for justice as this is contrary to the spirit of Islam.

Ibn Khaldun, therefore, elaborated on what he meant by *'asabiyyah* to avoid it from going against the teachings of Islam. The group feeling or solidarity in Khaldun's thesis was the basis for human society and the most basic of its relationship, which he described as part of human nature. Upon achieving unity, the aim would be to seek political power. Historically, Islam was the force for forging group feelings for unity and was a catalyst for change. In order to succeed, the *'asabiyyah* practised by the group must be stronger than that of the opponent. For instance, in GE14, the *'asabiyyah* of the incumbent UMNO/BN was in disarray due to weak leadership and corruption as compared to the opponent's coalition led by the former Prime Minister (PM) who presented a positive image for change. This resulted in the incumbents losing their seats in urban and non-Muslim constituencies; hence, the government lost power.

What is *'asabiyyah* and what it is not would be the best way to answer the question whether *'asabiyyah* is relevant and practical in contemporary politics. Ibn Khaldun encapsulated his meaning by stating that there must be some factors to cause a desire for cooperation to exist on a larger scale among human beings than among others (Sümer 2012). This word taken from a classical usage was then given a positive twist from its tribal context to a political force. Mohammed Talbi (as cited in Garrison 2012), on the other hand, contends that *'asabiyyah* is "at one and the same time the cohesive force of the group, the conscience that it has of its own specificity and collective aspirations, and the tension that animates it and impels it ineluctably to seek power through conquest" (Lawrence 2005: xv; Garrison 2012). It is not right to leave *'asabiyyah* at the point of tribal cohesion, as the ultimate objective is to gain power. In fact, it was due to the principle of strong *'asabiyyah* that UMNO was able to lead the country from independence in 1957 until 9 May 2018. This was also the case with the Malay Sultans in Peninsular Malaysia, who were given the semblance of absolute monarchs by the colonial government (The Pangkor Treaty of 1874 and the 'protectorate' scheme of the British limited the monarch's power). Upon independence in 1957, the Sultans agreed to the system of parliamentary democracy and constitutional monarchy. Ibn Khaldun stated that although ideal *'asabiyyah* should begin where there was blood relationship it was not limited to it. According to him, in the case of "clients and allies" they also shared the group's *'asabiyyah*. The key phrase he used was "*'asabiyyah* results only from blood relationship or something corresponding to it" (Ibn Khaldun 1967). Such keywords become fundamental to the study of the twenty-first-century world politics (Garrison 2012). In the contemporary situation of Malaysia, the leaders of UMNO/BN were able, even though they would not say so, to use *'asabiyyah* as a benchmark for collective identification where personal interests were willingly subjugated to the overall interests of the group to gain power. In other words, *'asabiyyah* was needed to inspire the struggle that encompassed a wider spectrum of human activities and was subordinated to the state. This is more than just a social cohesion but a commitment to sustain action (Arnason and Stauth 2004).

For Ibn Khaldun *'asabiyyah* was the fundamental factor "why people have common behaviour", and he discounted power, egoism, hedonism, social contract, language, religion, symbolic communication, instincts, individual psychology, learned behaviour and obedience to the cause (Osman 2004: 7). In order to operationalise the significance of *'asabiyyah*, at the state level, he introduced the concepts of *'umran* and *mulk* (political power) through group feeling or solidarity. In the *Muqaddimah*, he introduced the new science of civilisation/culture, *'ilm al- 'umran*. What is *'ilm al- 'umran*? There are many definitions of this term but Ibn Khaldun defined it as the general object of historical inquiry. Larousi Amri (2008: 359) describes it eloquently as follows: "Ibn Khaldun compresses this process in an engine of history which has an antecedent point (the state of being Bedouin) and a succeeding point (the state of being a town dweller)". To him *'asabiyyah* describes this process but "*'umran* is the finality which is always drawn from the process". While Monteil and Rosenthal translate the term as civilisation and Lactose interprets *'umran* as a total concept of economic, social and cultural activities (Arnason and Stauth 2004: 31), Fuad Baali (1988) translated it as the study of social organisation or civilisation or as the science of human association or the science of culture. Ibn Khaldun introduced history as a science—not as a narrative but as a record. His intention was to establish a new method of explanation and reasoning (Osmani and Nurullah 2009: 89–102). Ibn Khaldun's proposals following his own argument that society was not static but evolutionary, thus, the movement from *'umran badawi* (primitive civilisation) to urban *'umran hadhari* (advanced civilisation) seem to follow each other in sequence of "first to second or previous to subsequent, from the simple to the complex" (Amri 2008).

Here Ibn Khaldun considered the nature of society and social change, which made him say it is a new science of culture. In the *Muqaddimah*, he said, "this science … has its own subject, viz., human society, and its problems, viz., the social transformation that succeed each other in the nature of society" (Ibn Khaldun 1958: 77). His theory propagated when a social organisation was formed, it would result in *'umran*, which would lead to civilisation. According to Ibn Khaldun, as society and social organisation grew larger it would result in better *'umran*. Ibn Khaldun equated population growth to a corresponding growth in civilisation. In this regard, he believed that increase of population would culminate in the highest form of sedentary culture (Ibn Khaldun 2005). Ibn Khaldun assumed that progress meant a change from the *badawah* (primitive lifestyle) to the *hudarah* (advanced lifestyle). He took the position that nomadic tribes possessed better resilience, thus they had a stronger *'asabiyyah* (Kayapinar 2006). He distinguished civilisation of the settled people with the achievement in arts and crafts because they were self-sufficient while the nomads have to struggle for a living, hence they have physical and moral superiority over the city-dwellers. What he wanted to point out here is that these differences of conditions among people were due to the different ways they earned their living. In this regard, he made a comparison between different societies, to show their means of production that shaped their structures and historical limits (White 2009). He was able, in this way, to show that everything followed economic imperatives, as human society became more complex, production techniques would become more sophisticated and there would be greater division of labour.

Ibn Khaldun (1958: 136) concluded that, "the life span of a dynasty corresponds to the life span of an individual; it grows up, passes into an age of stagnation and thence into retrogression". Using this theory, it could explain the various processes in the growth and decline of UMNO when the state reaches '*umran*. He stated that every society ultimately would go through the experiences of "senility", which was beyond remedy because according to him, it was "a natural phenomenon and natural things do not change" (ibid., 137–138). Has UMNO gone to a stage of senility? In sum, this is the inevitable cycle of development. However, these cycles are not similar in all cases since all societies have their differences and are governed by the dynamics of continual change in their own environment (White 2009; Kayapinar 2006).

Ibn Khaldun believed when societies are transformed to being urbane as a result of development and, hence, more civilised, and they begin to enjoy the taste of comfort and luxury, the values of '*asabiyyah* like the nomadic or rural life disappear or become diluted. '*asabiyyah* breaks down due to massive urbanisation, dramatic demographic changes, a population explosion, large-scale migrations to the cities, the widening gap between the rich and poor, inter and intra ethnic groups, widespread corruption, loose governance and mismanagement of government leaders, political or otherwise. Additionally, globalisation, modernity, colonisation of the minds, culture and knowledge from the West as well as technological advancements have changed and challenged traditional values and customs. A large percentage of the Malay population is young, lack education competitiveness and are unemployed; therefore, they could easily be mobilised for radical changes (Imam 1978). The concepts he introduced and analysed co-relate to the current challenges and problems that many consider could be applied to the modern day social and political phenomena.

This study is enriched by the great number of existing literature by contemporary scholars on politics and social change as expounded by Ibn Khaldun, which enabled the researcher to draw assumptions and conclusions looking for its practical application. However, here the researcher's intention is to examine which principles in his political thoughts and theories could be adapted to the current political situation in Malaysia in order to comprehend the decline of political power and dominance of the UMNO in the Malay society and the country. The loss of *mulk* and the decline of dominance of UMNO/BN in GE14 could be assigned to the leadership's weaknesses, changing values, norms and customs of the urban population, which was not anticipated by the leaders of the government and the political parties. In examining the various challenges faced in the diverse society of Malaysia by UMNO, it is appropriate to seek answers from Ibn Khaldun's '*asabiyyah* and '*umran*.

Ibn Khaldun's theory is dynamic and applicable to universal and specific situations and environments and is, therefore, applicable to the political episodes and incidents happening in Malaysia today. It is interesting to note that scholars like E. Rosenthal and Kamil Ayyad questioned Ibn Khaldun's position regarding religion and practical philosophy. However, to secularise Ibn Khaldun would not be fair and right. In the *Muqaddimah*, he repeatedly stressed the need for seeking protection and guidance from God (Ibn Khaldun 1958). The researcher believes the way he dissociated himself from philosophy was with a view to indicate he was religious and a firm believer of the *naqli* or the acceptance of the teaching that not everything can be explained by reason or logic but remains in the realm of divinity. It is a clear indication he accepted what Allah (*s.w.t.*) has ordained for human beings such as in his discussion of social development and civilisations (*'ilm al- 'umran al-bashari*). He combined his intellectual prowess and religious beliefs in a very balanced manner.

Today, UMNO, due to decadence, is facing decline in its political power and dominion in Malaysia. Of course, no single factor can be assigned to the decline but moral and ethical disintegration is the primary cause for what I believe was the lack of solidarity and unity. Given the aforesaid premise, Ibn Khaldun theory of *'asabiyyah* is still relevant for UMNO if it wants to bring back group feeling and solidarity and regain its political power and dominance.

## 1.7  Organisation of the Book

There are a number of rationales for this study to unravel the concepts on which the edifice of the United Malays National Organisation (UMNO) was built. Firstly, this research examines the unique theory of Ibn Khaldun's *'asabiyyah* and *'umran* in the contemporary period in relation to the erosion of political power and dominance of UMNO on the Malaysian political scene. The theory of *'asabiyyah* and *'umran* have been studied and researched extensively by scholars and academics from differing perspectives to show they are similar or different from contemporary theories of history, politics and sociology.

However, in this research, the issue of examination is not in the generalities but specifically focused on the social transformation brought by *'umran*, hence the loosening of solidarity or *'asabiyyah* within the Malay Muslim society that has impacted UMNO. Contemporary scholars have agreed that Ibn Khaldun's theories of *'asabiyyah* and *'umran* are applicable to the past, present and possibly future rise and decline of societies and states. There is a resurgence of interest of contemporary scholars to study the nature and causes of the changes of societies and civilisations as discussed in the *Muqaddimah* though the numbers are still small. Hence, this research could add value to the corpus of knowledge and fill the gap on the applicability of Ibn Khaldun's political theory to the UMNO dilemma.

Secondly, most of the writings on Ibn Khaldun were comparative studies with contemporary western political and social theories be it modern or medieval times. As the term *'asabiyyah* is controversial and very much associated with the pre-Islamic tribal practice in Arabia, which was condemned by the Prophet Mohammad (PBUH) and resonates a negative connotation among Muslim Malaysians (includes non-Malay Muslims), this research will show that the natural *'asabiyyah* in the *Muqaddimah* is not inconsistent with Islam and its teachings in the Qur'an and Sunnah. Scholars like Caksu (2007), Kayapinar (2006), Alatas (2006a, b), Goodman (1972) and Gibb (1933) among others dealt with the theological and religious aspects of *'asabiyyah.*

Thirdly, it is significant in understanding the operationalisation of Ibn Khaldun's theory of *'asabiyyah* and *'umran* to the decline of political power and dominance of UMNO and its leaderships of Malaysia from GE12 in 2008 until GE14 in 2018.

UMNO could not sustain the hegemony of the Malay community or even the imagined communities from the aspects of state parochialism, Islam and nationalism (Anderson 1983). This theory of imagined communities could be implied to be applicable to the birth of Malay nationalism led by UMNO. This research would examine whether Ibn Khaldun's theory of *'asabiyyah* and *'umran* would be relevant to UMNO today and how it could be applied. Therefore, the significance of this research would be examining the factors for the decline of UMNO and how it could be overcome to answer the questions raised in this research.

Research design is the backbone of the entire research process. The problem statement defines independent and dependent variables related to the study and they are well-established. The research fits well into a descriptive and interpretative qualitative research design. The researcher primarily employs the qualitative research method in order to achieve the objectives of the study. This research utilises a variety of primary and secondary sources to develop the findings and conclusion. Since the research is predominantly library-based, both primary and secondary sources are collected mainly from the IIUM library, the National Library of Malaysia and libraries from other Malaysian universities. The researcher generally relies on primary sources such as authentic English translations of the *Muqaddimah* (*Prolegomena*) and other scholastic works on Ibn Khaldun's political and sociological theories. As secondary sources, the researcher utilises books, academic journals, articles and microfilms. Moreover, numerous online search tools such as A-Z Journals, ProQuest and the like are also used for collecting both primary and secondary material.

This research intends to analyse the decline of political power and influence of UMNO as the dominant political force in the government and Malaysian society by analysing the representations in the state assemblies and, at the federal level, in the parliament. The researcher focuses on the GE results of 2008, 2013 and 2018. This study uses official documents and conducts semi-structured interviews with political figures from UMNO and other relevant political parties to investigate the reasons for the decline of UMNO's political power. This study comprises five chapters as follows.

# References


Ahmed AS (2002) Ibn Khaldun's understanding of civilizations and the dilemmas of Islam and the west today. Middle East J 56(1):20–45

Ahmad Z (2003) The epistemology of Ibn Khaldun. Routledge Curzon, London

Alatas SF (2006a) Ibn Khaldun and Muslim reform: toward a conceptualization. Turkish J Islam Stud 16:782–795

Alatas SF (2006b) A Khaldunian exemplar for a historical sociology for the south. Curr Sociol 54(3):397–411

Alatas SF (2013) Ibn Khaldun. Oxford University Press, Oxford

Amri L (2008) The concept of *'umran*: the heuristic knot in Ibn Khaldun. J North Afr Stud 13(3):351–361. https://doi.org/10.1080/13629380701844672

Anderson B (1983) Imagined communities: reflections on the origins and spread of nationalism. Verso, London

Arnason JP, Stauth G (2004) Civilization and State Formation in the Islamic Context: Re-Reading Ibn Khaldun. Thesis Eleven 76(1):29–48

Arslan A (1987) İbn-i Haldu"un İlim ve Fikir Dünyası. Vadi Yayınları, Ankara

Azmeh, 'Aziz (2003) Ibn Khaldūn: an essay in reinterpretation. Central European University Press, Budapest

Baali F (1988) Society, state, and urbanism: Ibn Khaldun's sociological thought. University of New York Press, New York

Caksu A (2007) Ibn Khaldun and Hegel on causality in history: Aristotlelian legacy reconsidered. Asian J Soc Sci 35(1):47–83

Durkheim E (1997) The division of labor in society. The Free Press, New York

Edwards S. (2018). Reports: Malaysia's elections: Corruption, foreign money, and burying-the hatchet politics. 10 June. Al Jazeera Centre for Studies. https://studies.aljazeera.net/en/reports/2018/06/malaysias-elections-corruption-foreign-money-burying-hatchet-politics-180610090147666.html

Fromherz AJ (2011) Ibn Khaldûn: life and times. Edinburgh University Press, Edinburgh

Garrison DH (2012) Ibn Khaldun and the modern social sciences: a comparative theoretical inquiry into society, the state, and revolution. Master's thesis, University of Denver. https://digitalcommons.du.edu/etd/231

Gellner E (1982) Reviewed work: "Ibn Khaldun and Islamic thought-styles: a social perspective" by Baali, Fuad & Wardi Ali. Br J Sociol 33(2):295–296. https://doi.org/10.2307/589949

Ghazali AZ (2012) Persekutuan Tanah Melayu Merdeka, 31 Ogos 1957: Liku dan Jejak Perjuangan Patriot dan Nasionalis Menentang British. Persatuan Sejarah Malaysia Repositori Digital@PNM. https://myrepositori.pnm.gov.my/bitstream/123456789/3625/1/MDSS_2012_40_01.pdf

Gibb HAR (1933) The Islamic background of Ibn Khaldun's political theory. Bull Sch Orient Stud 7(1):23–31

Goodman LE (1972) Ibn Khaldun and Thucydides. J Am Orient Soc 92(2):250–270

Hodgson MGS (2009) The venture of Islam, volume 1: The classical age of Islam. Chicago: University of Chicago Press.

Ibn Khaldun (1958) The Muqaddimah: an introduction to history (trans: Rosenthal F), 1st edn. Princeton University Press, New York

Ibn Khaldun (1967) The Muqaddimah: an introduction to history (trans: Rosenthal F; abridged and ed: Dawood NJ) 2nd edn. Routledge & Kegan Paul Ltd. and Martin Secker and Warburg Ltd., London

Ibn Khaldun (2005) The Muqaddimah: an introduction to history (trans: Rosenthal F; abridged and ed: Dawood NJ; with a new introduction by Lawrence B) 3rd edn, Bollingen Series. Princeton University Press, Princeton and Oxford

Ibn Khaldun (2017) Ibn Khaldun on Sufism: remedy for the question in search of answers (trans: Y. Ozer. Cambridge: The Islamic Texts Society.

Imam SMA (1978) Some aspects of Ibn-Khaldun's socio-political analysis of history: a critical appreciation. Khurasan Islamic Research Centre, Karachi

Irwin R (2018) Ibn Khaldun: an intellectual biography. Princeton University Press, Princeton

Jason Wei JN, Rangel JG, Yet CP (2021) Malaysia's 14th General Election: dissecting the 'Malaysian tsunami'—measuring the impacts of ethnicity and urban development on electoral outcomes. Asian J Political Sci 29(1):42–66. https://doi.org/10.1080/02185377.2020.1814363

Kayapınar MA (2006) İbn Haldûn'un Asabiyet Kavramı: Siyaset Teorisinde Yeni Bir Açılım (Ibn Khaldun's Concept of Asabiyyah: a new expansion in political theory). Turkish J Islam Stud 15:83–114. https://dergipark.org.tr/en/pub/isad/issue/68676/1078999

Lawrence B (2005) Introduction to the 2005 Edition, in The Muqaddimah: An Introduction to History, translated by Franz Rosenthal. Princeton: Princeton University Press.

Kayapınar MA (2008) Ibn Khaldun's concept of Assabiyya: an alternative tool for understanding long-term politics? Asian J Soc Sci 36(3–4):375–407. https://doi.org/10.1163/156853108X327010

Mahdi M (1957) Ibn Khaldun's philosophy of history: a study in the philosophic foundation of the science of culture. G. Allen and Unwin, London

Moniruzzaman M, Farzana KF (2018) Malaysia' 14th general election: end of an epoch, and beginning of a new? Intellectual Discourse 26(1):207–228

Osman AS (2004) Hubungan antara Asabiyyah dan keruntuhan Kerajaan Baniumayyah: suatu analisis menurut Ibn Khaldun. Jurnal Intelek 2(1):54–61

Osmani NM, Nurullah AS (2009) Ibn Khaldun's Muqaddimah and 'Ilm Al-'Umran: an analysis. In: Bakar O, Ahmad B (eds) Proceedings of Ibn Khaldun's legacy and its significance. International Institute of Islamic Thought and Civilization ISTAC, Kuala Lumpur, pp 89–102

Ra'ees W (2004) Asabiyyah, religion and regime types: re-reading Ibn Khaldun. Intellectual Discourse 12(2):159–180

Ra'ees W (2013) Building Islamic polity within a secular framework of political activity in Egypt, Tunisia and Turkey with reference to Ibn Khaldun's theory of state. Al-Shajarah: Journal of the International Institute of Islamic Thought and Civilization 18(1):59–84.

Sümer B (2012) Ibn Khaldun's asabiyya for social cohesion. Electron J Soc Sci 11(41):253–267

UMNO Information (n.d.) UMNO History. Retrieved from UMNO Malaysia: https://umno.org.my/en/sejarah/

UMNO Johor (n.d.) Sejarah UMNO Johor. https://umnojohorofficial.wordpress.com/berita-terkini/w

Wan Teh WH (2017) Fasa Pertama Perjuangan UMNO Penuh Berani. Utusan Malaysia (UM). 11 May. https://wajabangsa.blogspot.com/2017/05/fasa-pertama-perjuangan-umno-penuh.html. Accessed 1 Aug 2022

Welsh B (ed) (2018) The end of UMNO?: essays on Malaysia's Dominant Party. Strategic Information and Research Development Centre (SIRD), Malaysia

White A (2009) An Islamic approach to studying history: reflections on Ibn Khaldun's deterministic historical approach. Intellectual Discourse 17(2):221–244

# Chapter 2
# Ibn Khaldun's Socio-Political Condition and Theory of *'asabiyyah* and *'umran*

**Abstract** This chapter discusses Ibn Khaldun's theory of *'asabiyyah* and *'umran*. Ibn Khaldun lived and experienced the decline of Muslim dominance in the early thirteenth and fourteenth centuries and wanted to understand the material cause of the eroding power of Muslims. Theorizing on the historical roots of the decline of Islamic civilisation, he argued that civilisation *'umran* is developed by human beings and the rise and fall of civilisations depend on what he called *'asabiyyah*. This chapter discusses Ibn Khandun's life, social-political and intellectual environment and his theory of *'asabiyyah* and *'umran*.

**Keywords** *'asabiyyah* · *'umran* · *'umran Badawi* · *'umran hadhari* · Ibn Khaldun's Socio-Political Conditions

## 2.1 Introduction

Ibn Khaldun lived and experienced the decline of Muslims dominance in the early thirteenth and fourteenth centuries. He wanted to find out the material cause of the eroding power of Muslims. In search of the historical roots of the decline of Islamic civilisation, he argued civilisation, *'umran*, is developed by human beings and the rise and fall of civilisations depend on what he called *'asabiyyah*. This chapter discusses Ibn Khaldun's life, social-political and intellectual environment and his theory of *'asabiyyah* and *'umran*.

## 2.2 Ibn Khaldun's Life

Waliyyuddin Abu Zayd Abd al-Rahman Ibn Muhammad Ibn Muhammad Ibn al-Hasan Ibn Muhammad Ibn Muhammad Ibn Jabir Ibn Muhmmad Ibn Ibrahim Ibn Abd al-Rahman Ibn Khaldun al-Hadhrami known to the world as Ibn Khaldun was born in Tunis on 1 Ramadan 732H/ 27 May 1332 CE. Ibn Khaldun had traced his



S. H. bin Syed Jaafar Albar, *Ibn Khaldun's Theory and the Party-Political Edifice of the United Malays National Organisation*, SpringerBriefs in Political Science,
https://doi.org/10.1007/978-981-19-7388-8_2

family's presence in Al-Andalus back to the Umayyad conquest of Iberia in the early eighth century. According to Y. Lacoste (1984), many historians in medieval North Africa and Al-Andalus noted the fame of the Banu Khaldun in Andalusian political, military and intellectual history; the male members of the family were well-regarded political advisors, religious scholars and generals. The Banu Khaldun had immigrated to Tunis from Al-Andalus after the fall of Cordoba and Seville (Lacoste 1984). Ibn Khaldun in his autobiography traced back his paternal roots to the companions of the Prophet Mohammad (PBUH), namely Wail Ibn Hajr. His family migrated to Seville during the Arab conquest of Al-Andalus. During the Reconquista of the Iberian Peninsula in the mid-thirteenth century, they went to Ifriqiya (Africa) and settled in Tunis during the rule of the Hafsid Abu Zakariyya (Calvert 1984; Esteban 2004). Ibn Khaldun's family had gained fame for excellence in politics and military service due to the long history of service in the Umayyad, Almoravid and Almohad dynasties of Al-Andalus. More important than his family's position and status, he was born in Tunis where the social, intellectual, cultural and political environment benefitted him. His nearest grandparent Abu Bakr ibn Muhammad ibn Khaldun (d. 737) became a trusted government officer of Amir Abu Yahya al-Lihyani, a provincial leader during his time. Ibn Khaldun's early years in Tunis coincided with the Marinid's ruler Abu al-Hasan struggle for power. In 1347, Abul al-Hasan successfully occupied Tunis and he brought along with him a large entourage of literary figures and religious scholars.

Ibn Khaldun's father was a scholar who arranged for him to acquire the best education. His earliest Islamic education was from his father and other famous Islamic teachers in Tunisia. In this regard, his father had a great influence on his education. Ibn Khaldun was educated under the influence of his father "who was his first teacher" (Enan 1979: 8). His learning of Qur'an and Islamic *fiqh* (jurisprudence) from Abu Abdillah Muhammad ibn Sa'd ibn Burral al-Ansari from Spain were extensive and covered many aspects of his life. In his autobiography, he acknowledged many of his teachers such as Abu Abdilllah ibn Al-Arabi al-Hasayiri, Abu Abdillah Muhammad ibn al-Shawwash al-Zarzali, Abu al-Abdas Ahmad ibn Qasar, Abu Abdillah Muhammad ibn Bahr, from whom he acquired the knowledge of Arabic poetry. According to Ibn Khaldun, he learned the basic concepts of philosophy, and logic, from the great logician Abu Abdillah Muhammad ibn Ibrahim al-Abili who influenced his intellectual development (Fromherz 2011).

Ibn Khaldun had a very stimulating intellectual environment and exposure at a very early age (Abdesselem 1960). Ibn Khaldun's life and career was interspersed between his interests in scholarship and politics. This obviously influenced his worldview of life itself. His career and travels could be discerned from the writings of his autobiography. Ibn Khaldun was born into a family where education and learning were given top priority. The fact that his family was among the nobles in the society meant he had easy access to political figures and scholarly discourses. Fischel (1967) and Syed Farid Alatas (2006a, b, 2007, 2013) suggested that Ibn Khaldun's life would be better understood if divided into comprehensible important phases (Wan Razali 2014). Fischel (1967) divided it into two phases, namely, the Maghreb (from birth to fifty years) and Egypt (four years until his death); while Alatas (2013) divided it into three phases (namely first phase of twenty years covering his continued education, the period 20 years when he was in political office), and his third phase of thirty one years where he served as a scholar, teacher and magistrate. In the first two phases he was in Spain, or Muslim west, and in the last phase between Maghreb and Egypt. There are other divisions or phases done by different scholars of his life such as Enan (1979), Rosenthal (Ibn Khaldun 1958), Schmidt (1978), Al-Ṭabbāc (1992), and Simon (2002). Wan Razali (2014) adopted the same approach and this researcher agrees.

### *2.2.1  Socio-Political Conditions*

Garrison (2012) has rightly argued that the historical descriptions of the political, economic, social and intellectual environments of fourteenth-century Maghrib would depend on the sources. In order to understand the relevance and significance of Ibn Khaldun's political thoughts and ideas, it is important to place them in the context of the socio-political conditions of his time. Lawrence (1983) and Lacoste (1984) as cited in Garrison (2012) say that during Ibn Khaldun's time, North Africa was relatively enjoying commercial prosperity, technological advancement and intellectual achievement. On the other hand, Nathaniel Schmidt (1978) had a different opinion on Ibn Khaldun. The researcher thinks Schmidt exaggerated the environment in Ibn Khaldun's time when he said the experiences and exposure he went through "took him to huts of savages and into the palaces of kings, into the dungeons with the criminals and into the highest courts of justices; into the companionship of the illiterate, and into the academics of scholars; into the treasure houses of the past and into the activities of the present; into deprivation and sorrow and into affluence and joy. It had led him into the depths where the spirit broods over the meaning of life" (as quoted in Ashraf 2015: 4). Hodgson's *"The Venture of Islam"* (1974) gives the socio-political situation of the region after the fall of the Almohad Empire in 1269 CE. He fairly and realistically depicted the period after the collapse of the Almohad Empire, which left and created isolated unstable emirates throughout North Africa and Muslim Spain then. The grandeur of the Empire was left as just a memory. The effect was that they could no longer focus their attention on sustaining their social, economic and intellectual activities; instead, they had to concentrate on defending themselves. Ibn Khaldun depicted the picture of the Islamic world during the fourteenth century as decline and disintegration set in (Mahdi 1957). Taking into account this depiction of his life, it goes to show Ibn Khaldun was confronted with continuous political intrigues and jealousies in his career and life but whatever action he took was for his survival. The changes of allegiance of Ibn Khaldun to different rulers and regions from Arab Spain to Syria often led to negative perceptions of him and led some modern scholars to criticise Ibn Khaldun as opportunistic, someone who lacked a sense of patriotism. In his over 30-year career, Ibn Khaldun shifted his allegiance frequently from one royal court to another (Marinid, Hafsid, Zayyanid and Granadan Empires) in order to survive (Lacoste 1984). However, the various intrigues and manoeuvres he experienced provided him new opportunities to study the dynamics of human social interaction and understanding of inter and intra state politics (Mahdi 1957).

Tunis unfortunately suffered when the Marinid rule came to an abrupt end and with it the flourishing intellectual centre as a result of the political power struggle and the Black Death in 1348 that swept the region. The Black Death killed his parents, all his teachers and many of his extended family members. Fromherz (2011) and Garrison (2012) said the plague dramatically impacted Ibn Khaldun's worldview on public sanitation, urban life and urbanisation and inspired him to write the *Muqaddimah*. Such compounding trauma no doubt had a lasting impact on his thoughts (Calvert 1984; Estaban 2004).

### 2.2.2  *Intellectual Environment*

With the death of his parents during the plague in Tunis and the departure of the Marinid rulers, Ibn Khaldun felt the emptiness of the intellectual environment of the city, while he still had a great thirst for learning (*Ta'rif*) (Abdesselem 1960). He was invited to go to Fez and he accepted it because Abu Inan, like Ibn Khaldun's father, promoted learning and scholarship in Fez. In Fez, Ibn Khaldun was able to meet, work and study with a large number of scholars. Ibn Khaldun joined the Sultan's *majlis al-'ilmi* (intellectual circle) and while serving in this position he was able to complete his education. Due to his family's wealth, privilege and political status, Ibn Khaldun had received the best education available, studying under the best teachers in North Africa in very diverse academic fields. He was fortunate that he studied outside the state-controlled system. His teachers gave him intellectual freedom and allowed him to have a broad-based education, which influenced his critical thinking and creativity. He was an interdisciplinary scholar. He learned the Qur'anic *tafsir* (exegesis), hadith collections, the fundamentals of Maliki *fiqh* (jurisprudence) and theosophy of Sufism. Beyond the religious studies, Ibn Khaldun also took lessons in literature, poetry, Arabic linguistics and foreign languages, biographical and historical sciences and academic writing. In addition, he was educated in the 'modern' Hellenistic subjects of mathematics, logic, natural philosophy and in metaphysics. He read Plato, Aristotle and the Stoics. In the Islamic philosophy, he was well-versed, *inter alia*, with the works of al-Farabi, al-Razi, al-Tusi, Ibn Rushd and Ibn Sina.

Thus, he was a person exposed to Islamic intellectual heritage as well as classical Greek philosophy, which inspired him in the academic pursuits as well as gave him the ability for critical and rational inquiry. The wide-ranging training he went through had a profound effect on the way he looked at knowledge and human capacity for rational and critical thought. It made the young Ibn Khaldun realise humanity's limitation and he began to discuss the 'phenomenon of prophecy' and man's relation with his Creator in a more systematic and scientific manner. This enabled him to be proficient in the fields of revealed (*naqli*) and rational (*aqli*) sciences. This could be clearly seen especially in his writings in the *Muqaddimah* and *Tarikh*.

Politics played an important role in Ibn Khaldun's intellectual works. In Fez, Abu Inan, the son of Abu al-Hasan appointed Ibn Khaldun as the state secretary, a post which he took up unenthusiastically. Ibn Khaldun is narrated in *Ta'rif* to have said that: "I devoted myself to reflection and to study, and to sitting at the feet of the great teachers, those of the Maghrib as well as those of Spain who were residing temporarily in Fez, and I benefitted greatly from their teaching" (Abdesselem 1960: 53–54). In his translation of the *Muqaddimah*, Rosenthal says that Ibn Khaldun (1958) was more focused on his desire to learn rather than on his position in politics. Nevertheless, he held this position for three years, as he was imprisoned for two years on the charge of conspiring to help the exiled Hafsid Amir of Bijaya, Abu Abdullah, to regain his throne. He went through many such allegations of intrigues and betrayals throughout his career as a scholar and politician/statesman serving under several rulers and princes of the Marinid, Hafsid, Ziyanids and Granada emirates. For Ibn Khaldun even though there were those who branded him as a dangerous opportunist, every new intrigue and political manoeuvre he went through allowed him a new exposure to understand better the dynamics of human social interactions and the inner workings of inter and intra state politics (Mahdi 1957).

Ibn Khaldun's wide exposure to palace politics provided him an insightful perspective and enabled him to critically analyse history, *mulk* (power and authority) to establish a kingdom and government/state and social change. Ibn Khaldun synthesised his experience of North African and Andalusian politics and collected data using his knowledge of classical and Islamic history to develop the historical principles of society and politics. Thus, based on his experiences and observations, are lessons and examples for contemporary as well as future leaders. His theory has been crafted in a manner that can be utilised for practical application (Fromherz 2011). However, he was a witness to the rise and decline of Islamic states and dynasties in North Africa and Spain. He observed how the Islamic populace and political organisations in Maghreb lost their political power and disintegrated into oblivion after ruling for a period of several hundred years. Ibn Khaldun in his investigation was keen to find answers to the following questions: why was Maghreb an unstable state? Why were there very few attempts made to reinstate the state to its *'umrani* position of peace, wealth and prosperity? And if there were such attempts, why did they end up in failure? Ibn Khaldun wanted to know why and how do empires rise and fall? What is politics all about and the purpose of government? How are civilisations built? Ibn Khaldun was confronted with these questions that made him study and write on the essence of human nature, social organisation and the driving force that motivates a society in a given situation.

Ibn Khaldun was a scholar who gained fame for his *Muqaddimah* where he expounded the philosophy of history and the theory of the rise and fall of civilisations (Campo 2009). He travelled extensively to different regions of Africa, Arabia and European countries such as Morocco, Spain, Egypt, Palestine and the Arabian Peninsula. His writings were based on his experiences and observations. In the *Prolegomena*, Ibn Khaldun presented his theory of *'ilm al-'umran* on social, historical development and the rise and decline of a society. His work enables historians to establish a benchmark in judging recorded events and social changes in historical reporting. Ibn Khaldun considered understanding the past history of mankind as significant to shape the present and plan for the future. For the first time, he propounded the methodology of history not being merely a recorded chronology of events, but as sociology. He took a different approach from Ibn Sina, Ibn Rushd and al-Ghazali in not focusing his attention to metaphysical, philosophical and religious issues; instead, he decided to discuss the challenges and problems of society and social sciences. Ibn Khaldun took a unique perspective by stating that his theory and conclusions are based on natural science. Even though it was difficult to draw a line between natural sciences and positive sciences or divine law, he introduced what he called as new "science of culture". He categorically emphasised that this science has never been done before and was premised on natural philosophy. His theory relates to the study of human society and the causes of its rise and fall. His sociology examined the present, which would shed light on history and the past. Using his experience and observations as a statesman, diplomat and politician who had travelled extensively, he had gained empirical evidence of the events and episodes in politics and history. He was, thus, able to study different forms of human society by investigating their nature and characteristics and examining how the evolution of human society took place.

According to Ibn Khaldun, a man could not live and purely survive as a self-satisfying individual; thus, he is very much dependent on his physical environment since he could not possibly be the producer and at the same time the supplier for all his needs. This requires him to be associated with others, hence, an individual has to live in a family, with a tribe or in a nation and cooperate with other human species. This phenomenon was how Ibn Khaldun introduced and explained how tribes or clans strengthened their bonds for safety and security as well as cement group feeling or social solidarity. Ibn Khaldun developed this behaviour of human beings into a political and social concept, whereby he believes that with the sense of *'asabiyyah*, there would be peace and political stability.

Ibn Khaldun confessed that he decided to write on history for the following reasons: (1) problematic and wrong facts by previous historians; (2) to rearrange historical facts and reflections; (3) to provide a focus on the history of the Arabs and Berbers of Maghreb including their early origin up to his time and finally (4) to make new commentaries on the evolution of civilisation, urbanisation, human social organisation and dynasty building. He was seeking answers on the subjects of human nature, social organisation and social change (Schleifer 1985). The result was his *Muqaddimah*, which made him famous among the classical and contemporary scholarship. Ibn Khaldun wrote his *Muqaddimah* in restful tranquillity away from Maghrebi politics. One can find Ibn Khaldun's theory of state, *'umran*, *'asabiyyah* and method of analysing of history, society, human nature and politics (Wan Teh 2017). It is interesting to note that Ibn Khaldun also incorporated in his voluminous book history of the Arabs, Berbers and Turks, i.e., *"Kitab al-'Ibar"* into the *Muqaddimah* after he travelled to Egypt and the Levant.

For Ibn Khaldun, two conditions for understanding of history are important, which he observed in his *Muqaddimah*: first, understanding the causes and nature of events.

Second, the information relied on must be correct and the sources verifiable. This is of paramount importance in order to distinguish between what is right information and what is wrong. Lenn Goodman (1972) said this demonstrates Ibn Khaldun's demand for clarity, realism and critical thinking. Ibn Khaldun avoids intentionally from applying traditional methods in his historical research and interpretations. He advocated that his *Muqaddimah* must be useful not only for his period but in the context of contemporary life. For him, to get the true lessons from history, the methodology of inquiry and understanding must change. He believed the inquirer must be critical in their examination of facts and in interpreting events, cultures and civilisations based on underlying realities. It was here that he introduces his science of culture (Mahdi 1957).

## 2.3  Ibn Khaldun's Theory of *'asabiyyah*

A precise translation of the term *'asabiyyah* into English is difficult. Therefore, scholars linguistically and etymologically use the original Arabic term and define it based on its functions and what the word conveys. Hence, *'asabiyyah* has been defined differently. Halim (2012: 14) outlines the origin of the word from different sources. She traces *'asabiyyah* from the root word *'asab*, which has the meaning of "to bind". For Baali (1988: 43), *'asabiyyah* literally means 'binding' which would reflect being bound to a group. *'asabiyyah* means 'tribal kinships' and 'the implication of the strengthening bond'. *The Arabic English Lexicon* (Lane 1968: 2059) gives more depth to the possible meaning of *'asabiyyah* by suggesting, "a person demonstrates group feeling when he feels angry and compelled to act in defence of his group". The same dictionary also says etymologically *'asabiyyah* has the literal meaning "of bounding the turban round one's head" (the turban could be a metaphor for the tribe and for the head, representing individual disposition but the former seems more likely). Thus, *'asabiyyah* incorporates the quality of an individual's "action in helping his people or group against any aggressive action against them whether they are wrongdoers or wronged and in protecting them".

Goodman (1972) says the root word of *'asabiyyah* means 'nerve' as in the 'fibre or sinew' by which a group is held together. *Lisan al-Arab* defines *'asabiyyah* as the request of mutual self-aid or cooperation. Rosenthal (1958) in his translation of *Muqaddimah* simply defines *'asabiyyah* as 'group feeling'. Monteil (1967) likens it to a sense of 'esprit de corps' or 'esprit de clan', while Durkheim (1997) was the first to use the term of 'mechanical solidarity' or 'organic solidarity'. He ascribed this to mean Ibn Khaldun's *'asabiyyah* is simply solidarity tout court (simple). Other scholars have given a variety of meanings depending on the circumstances and situations of its usage.

Hence, the meanings can be taken in different contexts, to mean 'group consciousness', *'gemeinsinn'*, 'national *itatsidee'*, 'corporate spirit', 'feeling of solidarity', 'group solidarity', 'group will', 'communal spirit', 'social cohesion', 'martial spirit', 'striking power' and 'social solidarity'. All meanings of *'asabiyyah* demonstrate the presence of commonality of objectives to form a collective will to cooperate for a certain specific objective. Having examined the meaning and definition of this theory, this study attempts to show that the Malay society in its struggle against colonial rule and for independence used race, religion and nationalism to create group feeling and solidarity. It was an exemplary quest of developing an agro-based nation beginning with a rural economy to become an 'umranic state that enjoys peace and economic growth by democratic means. The country achieves industrial growth, a peaceful environment, political stability and social development (discussed in Chapter 3).

Whatever definitions or contexts one applies to define the term, traditionally the word and practice of 'asabiyyah is frowned upon in Islam but on further examination Prophet Mohammad (PBUH), as reported by Abu Dawood as authentic hadith, has not categorically forbidden it. It is narrated that Prophet Mohammad (PBUH) has pronounced that "helping your own people in an unjust cause" and "He is not of us who proclaims the cause of tribal partisanship and he is not of us who fights in the cause of tribal partisanship; and he is not of us who dies in the cause of tribal partisanship". When his companions asked him to further explain about the meaning of 'asabiyyah (tribal partisanship), he (PBUH) explained that "(It means) helping your own people in an unjust cause" (Asad 1961). Premised on the complete reading of the Prophet Mohammad S.A.W.'s tradition, it would not be wrong to say the natural 'asabiyyah of Ibn Khaldun coupled with religion and justice is not contrary to Islamic teachings.

### 2.3.1   Formation of 'asabiyyah and Its Dynamic Role

'Asabiyyah was formulated to bring group feeling and solidarity of a tribe on the basis of blood or clan relationships. Later on, it expanded to include any group or allies with a common objective to assert itself for political power and authority. Ibn Khaldun holds the view that 'asabiyyah is an inevitable phenomenon in constructing the human society. He considers the human species to have a natural tendency to establish grouping as a collective endeavour to cooperate with each other. He further added in order to strengthen the sense of 'asabiyyah, it has to be complemented by the practice of religion and the sense of justice. He argued that 'asabiyyah will not drift away from its natural purpose of serving the interest of the whole group and collectively of men when guided by religion and justice. 'Asabiyyah corrupts and drifts away when selfishness and individualism of the leaders and its group members and elites is its guiding force. Chances of social corruption and injustices increase. Here, alliances and groups formed will promote the selfish interests of certain individuals at the expense of the common good.

Ibn Khaldun turns 'asabiyyah into a political concept in understanding social organisation, civilisation and rise and fall of states/dynasties. For Ibn Khaldun, the term has a positive meaning or connotation. He defines it in a way that would not be contrary to the teachings of Islam contained in the Qur'an and Prophet Mohammad's traditions. Ibn Khaldun considers it as an essential attribute of human beings (human nature) to live together in a group/community; hence, for him, society is a natural outcome and a necessity. Thus, *'asabiyyah* becomes a political and social tool to work together to achieve solidarity and, with it, unity for a common and shared objective to establish an organised political society, to bind together for defence, agricultural and industrial fulfilments. He develops the economic concept of dependency and complementarity in society or group, for the exchange of resources or production for supply to the needs of other members of society. *'Asabiyyah* is a necessary prerequisite for all social relations and the driving force for cultural, intellectual and economic development. Ibn Khaldun, however, considers *'asabiyyah* to have its own cycle of ups and downs whenever group feeling and solidarity erode, which would enable a new group with a stronger *'asabiyyah* to assert itself and gain political control and dominance for *mulk*.

In Ibn Khandun's view, *'asabiyyah* interacts with *'umran* through five stages and move society and life towards *'umranic* lifestyle or causes the decline of *'umranic* life. They are: (1) Conquest: this is based on strong feelings of *'asabiyyah* that produces an irresistible strength among the tribesmen; (2) Single ruler: emergence of a charismatic, respected leader; (3) Broadly popular rule: the period when the leaders draw strength from the group; (4) Over-confidence: the ruler becomes complacent and cuts off his relationship with the majority of the population. The ruler becomes reclusive and surrounds himself with most loyal servants. Population has become sedentary and accustomed to the luxuries of city life; and (5) Collapse: new underdog tribal group seizes control. Their togetherness gives them the edge; *'asabiyyah* exists in every stage but the degree of its effectiveness varies from high to low. It is interesting to note that Ibn Khaldun connects the degree of effectiveness of *'asabiyyah* with political leadership. The stronger and just the leader of a community is, the stronger and durable the *'asabiyyah* and the *'umran* would be. When *'asabiyyah* is high or strong, society moves towards the *'umranic* stage of its development but the *'umranic* phase of life erodes when *'asabiyyah* begins to decline. The reason for the decline of *'asabiyyah* and the subsequent fall of the *'umranic* lifestyle is the complacency of the political leadership. When leaders become complacent and become engrossed in unfair and corrupt practices, *'asabiyyah* declines and *'umran* collapses.

Ibn Khaldun, in the *Muyuddimah*, also described the process of transformation of rural to an urban society with economic growth and civilisational progress, changing the lifestyle, wealth, prosperity, luxury and comfort of the people. But Ibn Khaldun believed that *'asabiyyah* was stronger in the nomadic phase, and decreased as civilisation advanced. The decades from the late 1990s up to date in Malaysia are identical to Ibn Khaldun's full *'umranic* conditions. The then ruling government of Malaysia and the ruling party went through serious slippages in terms of freedom, governance, corruption and public accountability. The society becomes more liberal and individualistic and its sense of solidarity and unity becomes relaxed. Tibi (1997) opines that when the sense of *'asabiyyah* declined, another more compelling *'asabiyyah* may take its place; thus, civilisations followed through rise and fall, and history describes these cycles of *'asabiyyah*' (this point helps to explain the decline of political power of UMNO discussed in Chapter 4).

For his case study, Ibn Khaldun used the Bedouin community as a reference point to show how *'asabiyyah* was formed to make the tribe stronger and felt superior than the others. The unity and solidarity brought by *'asabiyyah* among the Bedouins (*badawa*) enabled them to defeat urban or sedentary people (*hadara*) who were settled in towns and cities due to the loosening of their *'asabiyyah* or group feeling. Upon victory, the *badawa* group would obtain *mulk* and establish political institutions of the state/dynasty to administer the polity/city. This cycle in terms of social development, subsequently with *mulk* establishing their state that has wealth and prosperity, enables the new urban dwellers to enjoy life, and experience luxury and comfort of sedentary life. The sense of *'asabiyyah*, under these circumstances, according to Ibn Khaldun, is weakened when the *hadara* group becomes complacent and individualistic, and fails to practise good governance and tolerates corruption. This will cause the decline and ultimately the collapse of the state or dynasty.

### 2.3.2  *The Key Feature of* 'asabiyyah

The aim of *'asabiyyah* is to acquire *mulk*. *Mulk* at once embodies the state structure and the institutions under it. Therefore, the fundamental feature of *'asabiyyah* is that it is considered as the engine that drives power and exercise of authority through state institutions. In this way, one can understand the relationship that exists between society, religion and state as a consequential process. Ibn Khaldun believed that power and authority could be fully realised if the binding force, i.e., *'asabiyyah* is legitimate. State and exercise of power become legitimate when *'asabiyyah* is legitimate and *'asabiyyah* in Ibn Khaldun's view draws its legitimacy when political leaders gain the peoples' or tribes' support when they propagate religious ethos and promote justice for all members of the community. Ibn Khaldun said that the *badawa* people lived in remote areas of the desert with very harsh environment and conditions, which drove them to cooperate and stay together for survival against harm from all kinds of external threats. The *'asabiyyah* or group feeling was the cementing element to keep them together and strong. Hence, *'asabiyyah* was the binding force for the group feeling and solidarity to ultimately gain and maintain *mulk* and the state, or perhaps in Ibn Khaldun's words royal authority. It is necessary to note that Ibn Khaldun did not advocate a specific form of state, i.e., monarchic, democratic or theocratic. In Ibn Khaldun's opinion, state draws its legitimacy from its purpose, which constitutes the basis of its material cause, i.e., *'asabiyyah*. And the purpose of state which *'asabiyyah* aims to achieve is justice and public interest and the well-being of the citizens. But, *'asabiyyah* will lose its legitimacy and will wither away and the group's hold onto power will disintegrate when political leaders abandon the purpose of formation of *'asabiyyah* and the formation of state and exercise of power. Ibn Khaldun opined that when the political elite begins to abuse and misuse power and state institutions are used to promote parochial selfish interests of small group of individuals, then public interest and the well-being of the citizens are given lip service attention. Citizens feel disillusioned and disenchanted and begin to withdraw their support of the political leaders and the state in favour of another set of elites whom they feel can serve their interests. In this way, the *'asabiyyah* weakens, the political elite loses legitimacy and eventually loses *mulk*, that is the hold on power and control of state. (The decline of *'asabiyyah* in the case of UMNO and its removal from power in 2018 is discussed in Chapter 4).

## 2.4  Ibn Khaldun's Theory of *'umran*

The two most important translations of *'umran* are 'culture' and 'civilisation'. Some scholars chose culture while others would prefer to translate it as civilisation. For the purpose of this research, the researcher uses civilisation. The *Muqaddimah* is about 1200 pages thick, which reflects the importance Ibn Khaldun attaches to the knowledge of *'umran* as precursor to the study of history (El-Rayes 2008: 8). Ibn Khaldun's (1958) reason for giving so much attention to *'ilm al-'umran* (science of civilisation) is to indicate that the subject is a new science. Ibn Khaldun claimed that no scholar before him ever attempted to deal with the subject of the science of *'umran.*

Edward William Lane says that the word *'umran* is derived from the Arabic verb-root *'-m-r* that literally means "he aged", "he grew old", "he lived" or "continued in life" (Ungar 1958, as cited in Lane 1968). However, according to the authoritative Arabic Lexicon, "*Lisan al-'Arab*", the substantives of *'-m-r* (i.e., *al-'amr, al-'umur,* and *al-'umr*) all signify life (*al-hayat*). Based on this verb-root, El-Rayes says it points to the idea of growing up or getting old. In this manner, one is aware that one's span of life as human beings is limited. El-Rayes in his thesis (2008: 14–15), says that among contemporary Arabic speakers, the word *'umran* would mean something like "building" or perhaps "a place flourishing with human activity". Ibn Khaldun uses the word *'umran* to denote human grouping, human flourishing, as well as an organising standard that makes this formation possible. The term, therefore, relates to the studies on the development of society or human social organisation (*al-ijtima al insani*) in all its phases, beginning as a nomadic state to an organised state with the emergence of a sedentary lifestyle until its decline (Ibn Khaldun 1958). In the opening line of the *Muqaddimah,* Ibn Khaldun made it clear that a human being is very much a societal being, hence he cannot live on his own without society. It is his contention that *'umran* is a by-product of human cooperation and this allows the human species to live his natural life span. Albeit religion and history, Ibn Khaldun tells us, *'umran,* like all things, no matter how long they last, cannot exist forever. The life span (*'umur*) of a human being definitely has a beginning and an end. In this context, the principal object of Khaldun's science of *'umran* is to show the process in the cycle of growth, maturity and decline of societies.

Enan (1979) says the doctrine of *al-'umran* can be defined as sociology. Mahmoud Dhaouadi (1990; 2005) defines *'umran* as a philosophy of history, social philosophy or the science of civilisation. Ibn Khaldun defines *'umran* as the science of human civilisation (*'ilm al-ijtima' al-bashari*)) or the science of human society (*'ilm-al-ijtima' al-insani*). Both Amri (2008) and Enan say the concept is used primarily in and about studies of development of a society from its nomadic condition, to an organised state living in a sedentary or urban life, and moving from the phase of its rise to ultimate decline. Süleyman Uludağ argues that Ibn Khaldun in the beginning of the *Muqaddimah* denoted that the origin of the meaning of the Arabic word *'umran* is a condition of being developed and flourishing town (Ibn Khaldun 2020). From the aspect of language, the term *'ilm al- 'umran* originated from the root word *'amara* and *'amura* which has the meaning of "affluence" and "prosperity". This is justified if it is viewed from the wider perspective of its meaning, "a land, or house, inhabited, peopled, well peopled, well stocked with people and the like, in a flourishing state, in a state the contrary of desolate or waste or ruined" (Lane 1968: 2155). Edward William Lane says it also has the meaning of *bunyan* or "a building, a structure, an edifice" or perhaps the act of building" (Lane 1968: 2156). On the other hand, the terminology of *'umrani* has the meaning of "cultural, civilisation, serving or pertaining to ... cultural development" (Cowan 1974: 643); in the circumstance, it can be taken to mean something relating to development of a society or civilisation.

Amri crystallises the concept of *'ilm al- 'umran* further and says that it is the science what is called today 'sociology', the science of 'being together' and the science that is concerned with how to fill the empty space, that is to say, to occupy the land, to bring life to a territory and to establish urban groupings, including the founding of a town. The *'imara* is a building, an edifice, a construction, located in a population centre. One can also leave the space and look for correspondences through time such as the term *'umr*, the age of a person, a human being, a natural element. Age is depository of life. There is an apparent subjectivising of meaning, an apparent relativising of the sciences of living beings, a sort of restriction of life to a part, a segment, a little piece fused with death, but passed by birth and the emergence of new generations (Amri 2008). Amri contends that "the etymology of the linguistic stem in the Arabic Language refers to *'umran* as the fact of filling an empty space. But it can also have a semantic meaning referring to a contribution we bring to nature, that is to say, culture" (Amri 2008: 354). Wahabuddin Ra'ees (2004) argues that *'umran* is referred to as culture that becomes human product and is acquired and produced as a result of human relations.

From the above discussion, it is safe to infer that when *'umran* is viewed as culture, then it encapsulates state, political institutions, policies, norms, etc. When it is viewed as a human product, then it is produced only when human beings come together, interact and cooperate. It is not produced by a single individual in isolation but many must come together and agree unto it. Therefore, it is the feeling of coming together that becomes the real force behind human beings to develop and produce *'umran*. Ibn Khaldun said this group feeling exists when people see a shared objective or purpose in coming together. Ibn Khaldun called this group feeling *'asabiyyah* and, therefore, the material cause of *'umran* is *'asabiyyah*. State, organisations, policies, institutions, powers are constituent elements of *'umran* or cultures are produced by *'asabiyyah* or group feeling among citizens of a given state or members of a given community. Closely connected is the issue of the rise and decline of *'umran*.

Therefore, *'umran* will only decline, dynasties will disintegrate and groups will be removed from power when the *'asabiyyah* of members who created the *'umran* weakens obviously due to abandoning of the pursuit of purpose of creation of *'umran* by the elites. So, *'umran* declines and people are removed from power when the leaders and the supporters part company. Citizens withdraw their support and part company from those in power. They believe that the leaders have become corrupt and begun to use the luxury of power for their own well-being and have abandoned promoting the common cause and well-being of the community. The followers feel betrayed, cheated and deprived from the benefits of state policies. The *'asabiyyah* disintegrates and *'umran* collapses. (erosion of power and dominance of UMNO as a result of the disenchantment of the Malays is discussed in Chapter 4).

Cheddadi (2005) makes an interesting observation about Ibn Khaldun's typology of *'umran*. Cheddadi's observation is relevant to the discussion of role of UMNO (in Chapter 3) in transforming the rural Malays and Malays' socio-political status and creation of urbanised Malays and Malay socio-political and economic class. Ibn Khaldun categorises *'umran* into two types: (1) primitive *'umran* or *'umran badawi* and (2) civilised *'umran* or *'umran hadari*. Cheddadi says modern equivalents of *'umran badawi* and *'umran hadari* are rural-urban typology of society. Rural-urban typology for Cheddadi denotes lifestyle, civility, the mode of land acquisition, town dwelling, economic disparity and solidarity of Ibn Khaldun's *'umran badawi* and *'umran hadhari*, respectively (Cheddadi 2005). Ibn Khaldun (1958) said both are formed for different reasons and each has its own features. For instance, people in *'umran hadari* are affluent, and they live in large cities that have a confluence of social interactions and economic activities. The surplus and diversity of products will attract greater number of people to cities. These are absent in the *'umran badawi*. The city also employs a professional army to protect it against external threats which make their commodities and life secure. In the *badawi* situation, they have to provide their own security. Leaderships in the case of *badawi* are based on loyalty and allegiance or *bai'ah* (oath of loyalty) to a prominent member of the community. During the *'umran badawi*, loyalty and adherence to order is more sincere and unconditional leaderships are not determined by law but by members of the community declaring their loyalty to a particular leader usually based on blood ties and the person's election as leader. In *'umran hadhari*, power and state administration under the *mulk* has to be governed by law or state force and there must be obedience to these rules. In *'umran hadhari*, the leader possesses a security mechanism to defend him and the state structure.

However, the decline of *'umran* will be due to the weakening of the sense of *'asabiyyah*, thus loosening group feeling, solidarity and/or unity. Ibn Khaldun believed that when society during *'umran hadhari* reaches the peak of its development and economic success, it seems to be living in a state of comfort and luxury, adversely affects its resilience and causing the decline and ultimately the collapse of the state. The decadence becomes imminent without strong religious bond and morality.

## 2.5  Conclusion

This chapter discusses Ibn Khaldun's life, family background and intellectual environment that contributed to his growth as a scholar, statesman, historian and philosopher. His exposure in holding many positions under different rulers in Muslim Spain and the Maghrib as well as his knowledge in Islamic subjects and Greek philosophy made him an exceptional person. He wrote on the history of the world in his *"Kitab al-'Ibar"* with an introduction chapter, the *Muqaddimah*, based on his personal involvement in the various episodes, intrigues, observations and experience. He developed theory *'umran* and the role played by *'asabiyyah* in the rise and fall of *'umran*.

This chapter serves as a precursor to the ensuing two chapters that apply Ibn Khaldun's theory of *'asabiyyah* and *'umran*. The case of UMNO's emergence as the most dominant political force in the political history of Malaysia due to the strength of its leadership and its subsequent decline after 61 years is brought about because of the weaknesses of the leaders, as argued by Ibn Khaldun on leadership and *'asabiyyah*, upon which the thesis is premised. *'Asabiyyah* is one of the most crucial elements influencing the rise and decline of an entity or community.

## References


Abdesselem AB (1960) S.v. "Ibn Khaldun". In: Gibb HAR, Kramers JH, Levi-Provencal E, Schacht J (eds) The encyclopedia of Islam. E.J. Brill, Leiden

Alatas SF (2006a) Ibn Khaldun and Muslim Reform: Toward a Conceptualization. Turk J Islam Stud 16:782–795

Alatas SF (2006b) A Khaldunian Exemplar for a historical sociology for the South. Curr Sociol 54(3):397–411

Alatas SF (2007) The historical sociology of Muslim societies: Khaldunian applications. Int Sociol 22(3):267–288

Alatas SF (2013) Ibn Khaldun. Oxford University Press, Oxford

Al-Ṭabbāc, UF (1992) Ibn Khaldūn: Fī Sīratihi Wa Falsafatihi al-Tārīkhiyyah Wa al-Ijtimāᶜiyyah. Mu'assasah al-Maᶜārif, Beirut

Amri L (2008) The concept of *'umran*: the heuristic knot in Ibn Khaldun. J North Afr Stud 13(3):351–361. https://doi.org/10.1080/13629380701844672

Asad M (1961) The principles of state and government in Islam. Gibraltar: Dar Al-Andalus. Middle-East J Sci Res 11(9):1232–1237

Ashraf MI (2015) Ibn Khaldun: the great Muslim theorist of socio-political science. https://www.academia.edu/19925990/IBN_KHALDUN_%20The_Great_Muslim_Theorist_of_Socio-Political_Science (accessed on 3 August 2019)

Baali F (1988) Society, state, and urbanism: Ibn Khaldun's sociological thought. University of New York Press, New York

Calvert JCM (1984) Ibn Khaldun and the orientalist historiography of the Maghrib. Master's Thesis, McGill University. https://dokumen.tips/documents/ibn-khaldun-and-the-orientalist-historiography-of-i-ibn-khaldun-and-the.html?page=1

Campo JE (2009) Ibn Khaldun, Abd al-Rahman ibn Muhammad. In: Campo, JE (ed) The encyclopedia of Islam. Facts of File, New York

Cheddadi A (2005) Recognising the importance of Ibn Khaldun. Interview, 11 November. France Diplomacy. https://www.diplomatie.gouv.fr/IMG/pdf/Cheddadieng.pdf

Cowan JM (1974) A Dictionary of Modern Written Arabic (Arabic-English). Macdonald and Evans Ltd, London

Dhaouadi M (1990) Ibn Khaldun: the founding father of eastern sociology". Int Sociol 5(3):319–335. https://doi.org/10.1177/026858090005003007

Dhaouadi M (2005) The Ibar: lessons of Ibn Khaldun's Umran mind. Contemp Sociol 34(6):585–591. https://doi.org/10.1177/009430610503400602

Durkheim E (1997) The division of labor in society. The Free Press, New York

El-Rayes W (2008) The political aspects of Ibn Khaldun's study of culture and history. PhD Dissertation, United States, College Park: University of Maryland

Enan MA (1979) Ibn Khaldun: his life and works. Kitab Bhavan, New Delhi

Esteban D (2004) Religion and the state in Ibn Khaldun's Muqaddimah. Master's Thesis, McGill University. McGill University's digital repository. https://escholarship.mcgill.ca/concern/theses/8910jv21p

Fischel W (1967) Ibn Khaldun in Egypt: his publications and his historical research (1382–1406). A study in Islamic historiography. University of California Press, Berkeley and Los Angeles

Fromherz AJ (2011) Ibn Khaldun: life and times. Edinburgh University Press, Edinburgh

Garrison DH (2012) Ibn Khaldun and the modern social sciences: a comparative theoretical inquiry into society, the state, and revolution. Master's Thesis, University of Denver. https://digitalcommons.du.edu/etd/231

Goodman LE (1972) Ibn Khaldun and Thucydides. J Am Orient Soc 92(2):250–270

Halim AA (2012) The application of Ibn Khaldūn's theory of Asabiyyah to the modern period with special reference to the Malay Muslim community in Malaysia. PhD Thesis, University of Birmingham

Hodgson MGS (1974) The venture of Islam: conscience and history in a world civilization. University of Chicago, Chicago

Ibn Khaldun (1958) The Muqaddimah: an introduction to history (trans: Rosenthal F), 1st ed. Princeton University Press, New York

Ibn Khaldun (2020) Mukaddime: İbn Haldun (trans: Uludağ S). Dergah Yayinlari, Istanbul

Lacoste Y (1984) Ibn Khaldun: the birth of history and the past of the third world. Verso, London

Lane EW (1968) An Arabic-English Lexicon, vol 2. Librairie Du Liban, Lebanon

Lawrence BB (1983) Introduction: Ibn Khaldun and Islamic ideology. J Asian Afr Stud 18(3–4):154–165

Mahdi M (1957) Ibn Khaldun's philosophy of history: a study in the philosophic foundation of the science of culture. G. Allen and Unwin, London

Monteil V (1967) Discours sur l'histoire universelle (Al-Muqaddima) - Traduction nouvelle, préf. et notes par Vincent Monteil. Commission internationale pour la traduction des chefs-d'oeuvre, Beirut

Ra'ees W (2004) Asabiyyah, religion and regime types: re-reading Ibn Khaldun. Intellect Discourse 12(2):159–180

Schleifer A (1985) Ibn Khaldun's theories of perception, logic & knowledge: an Islamic phenomenology. Am J Islam Soc Sci 2:225–231

Schmidt N (1978) Ibn Khaldun: historian, sociologist and philosopher. Universal Books, Lahore

Simon R (2002) Ibn Khaldun: history as science and the patrimonial empire. Akadémiai Kiadó, Budapest

Tibi B (1997) Arab nationalism—Between Islam and the Nation-State. Macmillan Press Ltd, London

Wan Razali WMF (2014) Al-Ashariyyah Menurut Ibn Khaldun: Sejarawan Dan Ahli Sosiologi Islam. PhD Thesis, Bangi, Selangor: Universiti Kebangsaan Malaysia.

Wan Teh WH (2017) Fasa Pertama Perjuangan UMNO Penuh Berani. Utusan Malaysia (UM), 11 May. https://wajabangsa.blogspot.com/2017/05/fasa-pertama-perjuangan-umno-penuh.html (accessed on 1 August 2022)

# Chapter 3
# Rise of UMNO in Malaysian Politics

**Abstract** This chapter discusses the history of establishment of UMNO and the factors leading to the rise and dominance of UMNO in Malaysian politics. The underlining factors that ignited Malay nationalism in the 1940s were the desire for unity and solidarity and the need to express their political views on important national issues. The Malays felt the need for a political platform to serve this purpose and during the Third Malay Congress held in 1946, it was decided that all the existing groups and associations be integrated into one national body; the UMNO, to fight for the rights and freedom of the Malays. This chapter examines the formation of UMNO, the leaders involved in its establishment, its rising popularity and achievements.

**Keywords** UMNO · Merdeka · Solidarity · Coalition · Third Malay Congress · NEP · *Malayan Union*

## 3.1  Introduction

This chapter discusses the underlining factors that ignited the Malay nationalism nationwide in the 1940s. Malays desired to seek unity and solidarity and express their political views on important national issues. The Malays imminently needed a political platform to serve this purpose. The Third Malay Congress in 1946 decided that all the existing groups and associations be integrated into one national body; the UMNO, to fight for the rights and freedom of the Malays. This chapter further examines the formation of UMNO, the leaders involved in its establishment, its rising popularity and achievements.

  35
S. H. bin Syed Jaafar Albar, *Ibn Khaldun's Theory and the Party-Political Edifice of the United Malays National Organisation*, SpringerBriefs in Political Science,
https://doi.org/10.1007/978-981-19-7388-8_3

## 3.2  The Establishment of UMNO: An Overview

UMNO, as a political party, has gone through several phases from its First President Dato' Onn Jaafar to Tunku Abdul Rahman followed by Tun Abdul Razak, Tun Hussein Onn, Tun Dr. Mahathir Mohammad, Tun Abdullah Ahmad Badawi and Dato' Sri Mohammad Najib bin Tun Abdul Razak in line with what is called the "Rahman Theory" (Rahman Theory is known in the UMNO circles at all levels and even by members of the public). Najib was the last UMNO President to hold the reign of power as PM under the BN government prior to the GE of 9 May 2018. The party has been shaped by the leaders of UMNO to create group feeling or *'asabiyyah* at the relevant time through an evolutionary process. No doubt, UMNO faced many challenges. It should be noted that the party started as a movement whose membership consisted of associations only. Later, when it was institutionalised, its organisational structure was established, it opened its membership to individuals as well. It evolved from a state-centric communal movement to a national political party. Before examining UMNO's establishment, it is important to learn about some of the underlying factors of the colonial history of the Malay states that began in 1874 (Pangkor Treaty).

Prior to the British intervention, Malaya did not exist as a single nation-state entity (Winstedt 1948). It was simply a different *'kerajaan'* (a polity based on the sovereignty of a *raja*) ruled by a *Raja* as a head of state who would rule over his subjects. The idea of *'kebangsaan'* (Nationality) did not exist. Furthermore, the idea of formation of UMNO should be traced to the reawakening of conservative pre-war Malay movements at the state and district levels, which at that time intended to form a national organisation (Funston 1980).

UMNO is described as *'Lambang Martabat Bangsa'* and, hence, the adage UMNO: the symbol of nation's honour; quite a fitting expression of symbolism and branding. UMNO represents the Malays, the majority community in a pluralistic country. According to Wan Ahmed (2010), UMNO proclaimed that its nationalist leaders had made sacrifices in upholding the Malay rights and freedom (Wan Ahmed 2010). In the subsequent pages, an overview is outlined illuminating the different stages of UMNO's founding and the role of its past leaders and other key players irrespective of their ideological orientations (from left to right wing) who had influenced the political history of Malaysia. The following pages demonstrate UMNO's evolution and institutionalisation.

Malaysia is a parliamentary democracy with a dominant party system. In a parliamentary democracy, political parties play an important role in the nation's politics and the winning party controls the executive and forms the government. UMNO being the dominant ruling political party, it is more pertinent to analyse and interpret developments within it. Additionally, it would help shed light on the political situation of the country at that time. The real political power was with UMNO since the founding of the Alliance and BN. The PM was UMNO's President and many cabinet ministers were UMNO members with non-Malay ministers from the component parties of the UMNO-led coalition. In 1955, UMNO formed and led the *Perikatan*

(Alliance) government. In 1974, a new UMNO-led coalition with political parties in Sabah and Sarawak joined BN. This historical change was made, in the words of the third President and Second PM, Tun Razak as a necessary movement to reduce outbidding and politicking, avoiding the reoccurrence of the 1969 racial conflicts, suggesting UMNO's accommodating attitude of non-Malay ethnic minorities into the body politics in Malaysia while perseveringly championing Malays' rights and freedom.

### 3.2.1 The Expansion of UMNO

In 1939, the indigenous Malay community faced numerous existential threats as the migrant ethnic groups were more sizeable than the Malays and the Malay economic position lagged far behind the non-Malays. Consequently, state-level Malay associations were formed with the primary aim of developing a common goal in the political, socio-economic and cultural spheres. Two associations, namely the Persatuan Melayu Selangor (Selangor Malay Association) and Kesatuan Melayu Singapura (Singapore Malay Union) organised a National Congress in Kuala Lumpur in August 1939, before World War II, to solidify the unity of the Malay race. At this Congress, all Malay associations were called to unite on a broad Pan-Malayan basis rather than focusing on the individual states (Roff 1967).

Pursuant to the First Congress, a Second Malay Congress that included representatives from Sabah, Sarawak and Brunei was held in December 1940. The Congress arrived at several proposals for the British government to undertake, which comprised: devising a plan for the economic development of the Malays; appointing a Malay officer in all overseas missions as Assistant Director of Education; and providing more opportunities in the English education for Malay students (Roff 1967). These demands were grounded on the special position of the Malays as recognised by the British. It was argued that British policy thus far had failed to help the Malays secure government appointments. Overall, the outcome of this congress did not contain any radical recommendation for a political programme. It was viewed as a measured congress since it was attended by western elitists or anglophile Malays. However, there were already signs of political consciousness from the participants, but it was filled with regional feelings and parochial Malay nationalism (Cheah Boon Kheng 1979; Roff 1967; Gungwu 1981). In the end, the resolutions of the Congress were disappointing because there was no consensus even on the definition of a Malay. According to Mohd. Basri (1992), although it was a failure, it provided a useful framework for future Malay political action.

On 1 March 1946, a Third Pan-Malayan Malay Congress was held at the Sultan Sulaiman Club, Kampong Bahru, Kuala Lumpur, to denounce the British proposal to implement its MU plan. The MU plan had not only created controversy but also caused a fundamental change within the Malay society in terms of the traditional relationship between ruler and subject (Stockwell 1979). In order to avoid rivalries between local and state movements, the Congress needed a towering personality to bring together everyone in a Pan-Malayan movement. With a successful track record as the founder and leader of *"Pergerakan Melayu Semenanjong"* (Malay Peninsula Movement), Johor, Dato' Onn Jaafar from the State of Johor fitted the profile perfectly. The state of Johor was recognised as having made the greatest political progress under his leadership. In support of Dato' Onn Jaafar, a Malay newspaper—the *Majlis*—suggested in its editorial that Dato' Onn with his track record and aristocratic heritage was the most qualified person to preside over a Pan-Malayan Congress. Thus, the Congress accepted the suggestion from *Majlis*'s editorial, and he was thereby elected as the Chairman of the Congress. This election followed the Malay tradition whereby personal authority and traditional status by virtue of his background and heritage were acknowledged.

One of the notable accomplishments of Dato' Onn was his ability to diffuse the anger of the Malays against the Sultans for giving approval to MU and entirely shifting the blame instead towards MU. Hence, his call for a Pan-Malayan Congress was approved unreservedly. The third Congress was held for four days and it was attended by 200 Malay delegates representing 41 associations and officially opened by the Sultan of Selangor (Stockwell 1979). According to Stockwell's account, the Congress considered two important agendas: firstly, how to organise the Malay National Movement (*Pergerakan Kebangsaan Melayu*) and secondly the organisation of the campaign against MU. Dato' Onn was elected to be the Chair of the Third Malay Congress in 1946. It was decided then that a movement named *"Pertubuhan Kebangsaan Melayu Bersatu (PERKEMBAR)"* which in English means United Malays National Organisation (UMNO) be formed. A working committee was appointed to draft a constitution for UMNO comprising Dato' Hj Abdul Wahab bin Tok Muda Abdul Aziz (Panglima Bukit Gantang, Perak), Dato' Nik Kamil bin Nik Mahmud (Kelantan), Dato' Hamzah Abdullah (Selangor), Zainal Abidin bin Ahmad (Za'ba) (Selangor) and Dato' Onn Jaafar (Johor).

At the Pan-Malayan Malay Congress on 11–12 May 1946, the UMNO Constitution was approved and, on that date, the party was officially born. Dato' Onn was elected as the First President and Panglima Bukit Gantang as the acting Secretary General. The election of the office bearers of UMNO such as Dato' Nik Kamil bin Nik Mahmud, Dato' Sri Nara Wangsa Abdul Rahim bin Dato' Musa, Dato' Haji Abdul Wahab bin Tok Muda Abdul Aziz (Dato' Panglima Bukit Gantang), Wan bin Md. Yusof (Panglima Kinta, Perak) reflected how the Malays retained their traditional hierarchy.

The Congress passed the following resolutions (Wan Teh 2017) (see original text in Bahasa Malaysia in the footnote).[1]

1. The Malayan Union Constitution is rejected and is considered unlawful because it did not obtain opinion and consent, through consultation with the Malay people, who are the indigenous and legitimate citizens of the Malay States.
2. The Malayan Union Constitution has given the same status to Malays, who are subjects of the Malay Rulers, and the ethnic Chinese and Indians, who are not even citizens as yet and came as temporary migrants or British subjects of the Straits Settlements of Singapore, Malacca and Penang.
3. The Malayan Union Constitution reduced the dignity and sovereignty of the Malay Rulers to just being the Head of Religion and Malay Customs of their individual states. The absolute sovereign to govern is given to the Governor at the State level and Governor-General at the Federation level.

This Congress was the expression of an uprising or revolt though peaceful means of the Malays concerning the British. UMNO's call for the withdrawal of the MU Constitution was successful and was replaced with the Federation of Malaya Agreement in 1948. This could be likened to a quiet revolution whereby power was taken over from the British and finally Malaya became independent on 31 August 1957 (Wan Teh 2017).

In order to have a better perspective of the background of how UMNO was formulated, we should examine the outcome of the three Malay Congresses wherein political initiatives were proposed. After World War II, there were many challenges encountered by the community as a result of the implementation of the colonial government policies. This very much involved the demographic change of the Malay states that resulted from large numbers of immigrant workers who were imported for the rubber and tin industries. Additionally, there was a serious impact in the introduction of the MU Constitution especially on the following: citizenship equality to foreigners (Indians and Chinese), turning the Malay states into a British colony and removing power from the Sultans. These actions and dire political situation drove

---

[1] *"Kongres Melayu Se Malaya membuat beberapa ketetapan seperti berikut:*

1. *Perlembagaan Malayan Union itu ditolak dan dianggap tidak sah kerana tidak pernah memperoleh pendapat dan restu, secara berunding dengan rakyat bangsa Melayu sebagai pribumi dan rakyat yang sah bagi negeri-negeri Melayu.*

2. *Perlembagaan Malayan Union meletakkan kedudukan orang Melayu sebagai rakyat baginda Sultan sama taraf dengan kaum Cina dan India yang belum lagi bertaraf warganegara dan hanya sebagai pendatang sementara atau warga Inggeris bagi mereka di negeri-negeri Selat iatu Singapura, Melaka dan Pulau Pinang.*

3. *Perlembagaan Malayan Union menurunkan martabat Raja-Raja Melayu yang akan bertaraf sebagai Ketua Agama dan Adat Resam Melayu di negeri masing-masing. Kuasa pemerintah sepenuhnya diberikan kepada Gabenor di peringkat negeri dan Gabenor Jeneral di peringkat persekutuan"*.

the Malay community to find a platform that could confront the challenges, and in so doing stimulated the establishment of UMNO.

The establishment of UMNO began with numerous social movements that arose from the state and district levels until it became a significant national political party. It should be noted that in Malay political culture leaders play a dominant role in the organisation or society. UMNO's formation was the product of the amalgamation of many associations and social groups who were conservatives and traditionalists in a political movement that the British found more comfortable to engage and interact with. UMNO originated from state-centred organisations existing prior to World War II which emerged from being '*kerajaan*' (a polity based on the sovereignty of a *Raja*) to that of '*kebangsaan*' (National). It is important to have an appreciation of how the upsurge of Malay political and ethnic consciousness became national that accompanied the MU, which developed into a collective identity. The associated solidarity was based on the concept of a community of equals in which different players agreed to hold to a common and shared end. As UMNO is a Malay party, it maintained the traditional behaviour, which is the patron-client relationship and loyalty to the ruling elite. Malay culture dictates that there must be elements of respect, courtesy, good manners among others in terms of relationships and these are integral parts of the Malay behaviour in their politics and allegiance (Mohd. Basri 1992). This requires the different players in the organisation to work together and cooperate for the realisation of a common goal to prevail.

The members of UMNO developed a collective identity with a common goal and ideology. The leadership of UMNO has an advantage because they came from the Malay elites and aristocratic class and, in the Malay political and social culture, the principles of loyalty, patronage, support and influence are owed and interwoven with each other. Solidarity or group feeling ('*asabiyyah*') of the Malays evolved with its own political culture for the acquisition of *mulk*. The political and ethnic consciousness of the Malays was a product of a political system and the life history of the individuals who made up the system (Mohd. Basri 1992). According to Mohd. Basri, traditions, leadership, religion and ethnicity shaped the Malay political behaviour dominated by UMNO.

The *Kesatuan Melayu Muda* (Malay Youth Association) with radical leaders like Ibrahim Yaakob, Ishak Hj Mohammad and Ahmad Boestamam who were waiting to oust the British and the Japanese during the occupation encouraged the development of political consciousness among the Malays (Abdul Wahid 1977). These radical groups wanted an independent Republic of Malaya, subsequently to be merged with their Indonesian brethren under a new country called Indonesia Raya. It could not be realised due to the sudden surrender of the Japanese.

The British and the elite Malay leaders of UMNO feared to compete with the growing influence from the social and political movements of other Malay groups whose approaches were perceived as radical and unfriendly to the colonial government. UMNO was seen by the British, Sultans and Malay elite class as a more moderate, traditional and feudal Malay organisation that was perceived to be more reasonable and suitable to negotiate for independence. The Rulers and majority of the Malay masses accepted UMNO's approach as the better one. Meanwhile, UMNO represented itself as a more moderate, traditionalist party that adhered to feudal traditions. Hence, all groups accepted UMNO to be the appropriate and chosen negotiator for independence. Wan Ahmed (2010) explains how the British portrayed themselves in the image of a colonial benevolent ruler. This was evidently well rooted with all segments of the Malay ruling class and she suggested it was because of this reason that UMNO formed a somewhat close and cordial relationship with the British. She also explains why UMNO was able to fast-track self-government and subsequent independence efforts earlier than expected.

Faithfully, UMNO represented the Malay position and, at the same time, was engaged with the British on many contentious issues. One of the issues mentioned was the withdrawal of the MU, which received widespread opposition from all quarters of the Malay community, including the Malay traditional leadership. Moreover, it was also strongly criticised by very senior colonial officers who had served in Malaya before the war. In an article written on 16 April 1946 and published by *The Times* London,[2] these senior colonial officials wrote that the MU plan was "in effect an instrument for the annexation of Malay States" (Wan Ahmed 2010: 22). Therefore, UMNO's claim that it acted in the interest of the Malays was well-founded. To attest to this, UMNO successfully organised and led protests against the MU in 1946.

Dato' Onn and his colleagues in *Persatuan Melayu Semenanjung Johore* condemned the British and the Malay rulers on the MU. The granting of citizenship to the economically dominant Chinese and Indians and their being part of the government would mean the extinction of the Malay race. In 1951, Dato' Onn who founded the UMNO came up with a surprising recommendation (knowing well UMNO was set up specifically to protect and defend Malay interests). He recommended that UMNO admit direct membership of non-Malays and suggested that the name of UMNO be changed to United Malayan National Organisation. Dato' Onn thought with his personal authority and clout as a founder of the party, the recommendation would be approved. Surprisingly, it was endorsed by the Executive Committee of UMNO but was rejected by members of UMNO at the General Assembly. Consequently, in that year, Dato' Onn resigned from UMNO and was replaced by Tunku Abdul Rahman, who later became the First PM of Malaysia. Evidently, it seemed Dato' Onn was persuaded by the British to open up UMNO as a condition to expedite self-government and independence.

When the British returned to Malaya at the end of World War II in August 1945, everything they did was wrong especially in their attempts to turn Malaya into a full-fledged colony from just a mere protectorate (*naungan*). The act of the colonial government was to undermine the position of the Malays (on citizenship) and their sovereignty (power of the Malay rulers) and full colonisation of the nine Malay states, which was an affront to their religion, Islam, leadership of the country and their identity (Miller 1965; Adib 2003).

---

[2] In support of those who opposed the MU a number of former senior colonial officials namely, Cecil Smith (Governor & High Commissioner), L. N. Guillemard (Governor & High Commissioner), E. S. Hose (Acting Chief Secretary, FMS), George Maxwell (Chief Secretary, FMS), Frank Swettenham (Governor), Richard Winstedt (General Advisor) wrote a letter to the editor of *The Times* London.

According to Cheah Boon Kheng (1988), the intention of the MU was to turn Malaya into a unitary state to be governed by a British Governor and equal citizenship given to both Malays and non-Malays on the so-called premise of fostering consciousness of a new Malayan identity. This plan was seen as an annexation and, of course, it was met with strong Malay condemnation, which was ignored. The formation of UMNO witnessed the change of Malay political attitudes from state-centred spirit to national consciousness and they had 'to change their allegiance from that of *kerajaan* (subject of the state ruler) to that of *Bangsa* and *Kebangsaan Melayu*' (Ahmad Farouk 2002).

This exhilarated the birth of patriotism/nationalism among the Malays under the banner of '*Kebangsaan Melayu*' (Malay Nationalism) and '*Hidup Melayu*' (Long Live the Malays) became the political ideology of UMNO. The forceful rejection of MU after being approved by the nine Sultans was not anticipated by the British government. Dato' Onn used very strong language by saying that the Sultans had betrayed the trust of the Malays. For the first time, it seemed the Malay political culture of loyalty and obedience had changed. At this time, the elites and the Malay masses were willing to express their dissatisfaction and anger (though politely) towards the Malay Sultans for giving their approvals to the MU. The aristocratic elites, who were initially protesting against *jus soli* in the MU constitution, were now angry when the white paper that was published in January 1946 showed the Sultans had signed the agreement. They considered the Sultans had 'sold out' the right of the Malays (Mohd. Basri 1992: 40). The Malay media openly wrote "Sultan-sultan kena mainkan" (the Malay Sultans had been hoodwinked), such as Cheah Boon Kheng (1988: 22–23). The Sultans, who had initially supported the MU, backed down and got themselves involved at the forefront of this Malay resistance. Subsequently, all the peaceful revolts of various segments of the Malay community made the British government realise it was impossible to administer Malaya without the support of the Malay community. This ultimately forced the British government to restore to the Malay Rulers their powers; and to the Malays, their special positions (Cheah Boon Kheng 1988). As mentioned earlier in this chapter, Malaysian power politics started with ethnicity when the British introduced the divide and rule policy and until today ethnic identity plays a crucial role, notwithstanding that the name of the political parties may give the impression of Malayanness/Malaysianness (Khoon 1985).

As a movement and political party, UMNO was initially seen as adamant against granting citizenship to the Chinese and Indian immigrants due to fear that their large numbers could affect the Malay survival as the indigenous and majority community. Malaya was made multi-racial by the British to satisfy its economic interest for cheap labour. Yet, in 1955, with the first election to establish a self-rule administration, it was the same UMNO under Tunku Abdul Rahman, the Second President of UMNO and the First PM of Malaya that cooperated in a political coalition with Malaysian Chinese Association (MCA) and Malaysia Indian Congress (MIC) called *Perikatan* (Alliance) in Peninsula Malaysia. Almarhum Syed Jaafar Albar (the auther's late father), who was an information officer at that time, related to me that though it was not so visible or obvious to the public, there was always cooperation between the Malay elite and aristocratic leaders of UMNO, the elite Chinese and Indian leaders and the British.

This view could be supported in the smooth transition from the colonial rule to the post-independent Malay rule led by UMNO nationalists. Similarly, it was also due to this cooperation that Sabah and Sarawak became independent within Malaysia. In 1974, under the Third President of UMNO Tun Razak, the Alliance was expanded to a new height with the formation of coalition with political parties in Sabah and Sarawak under BN on the ground of reducing politicking (Mauzy 1982) to reflect the political reality as Alliance was UMNO, MCA, MIC but BN includes parties in Sabah and Sarawak.

The Japanese occupation and British interference in the Malay states by forcibly implementing the MU on 1 April 1946 shaped the Malay political attitudes towards the British. According to Victor Purcell (1948), who was in the Malayan Planning Unit responsible for crafting the Plan, the MU was a product of a joint British and Chinese enterprise. The main objective of MU was to have the left-wing Chinese and western educated non-Malay elites to play the dominant political role in the Malay Peninsula (Mohd. Basri 1992); the Plan indeed was thwarted by UMNO and its leadership.

The intention of the MU was to change the political demography of Malaya by initially derecognising the status of the indigenous Malays under the pretext of creating a Malayan nation. Secondly, it was to usurp the power of the Sultans who would then become mere subjects of the crown and be replaced by the Governor. In other words, the set-up of the MU was colonisation rather than a protectorate system that existed earlier. This opened the eyes of the Malays to understand what the real story behind the quick surrender of Malaya to the Japanese was. History has pointed to the fact that Malaya was just abandoned without really being defended by the British. Taking leave from the Japanese experience, the Malays came to a realisation that the British were not that powerful after all. Hence, political attitudes of the Malays showed a change though they were nothing revolutionary or radical. UMNO was a serious player in this process of the evolutionary attitude shift of the Malays in the fight for their rights. There was anger and disappointment at the British government for refusing to retract the MU policy, even when many different segments of Malay society condemned the Plan. The MU came at a time after World War II where there was greater Malay political awareness in respect of its rights, responsibility and power consistent with what was happening in other parts of Asia and Southeast Asia.

During the Japanese occupation in World War II, racial tensions between Malays and Chinese were a bit high and Malay nationalism grew. The Malays were happy to see the return of the British in 1945 but the status quo could not be maintained and a desire for independence was further enhanced. According to Ariffin Omar (1999), the British took the Malays out of the discussion in formulating the plan to build a Malayan nation. Neither was there any attempt on their part at uniting the various Malay communities nor to get the Malays to view themselves as one nation. However, the Malays rejected and were not concerned with creating a Malayan nationality or even to have a united Malayan nation; hitherto UMNO did not include this as part of its ideology (Omar 1999).

In comparison to other nationalist political parties and movements in Southeast Asia, UMNO was viewed as different because it did not consider the necessity to fight for independence but instead it demanded continued British 'protection' (*naungan*) from the disparate entities (Omar 1999). Tunku Abdul Rahman, in his BBC radio interview, said Malaya was grateful to the British for conceding independence. This meant to the Malay leaders of UMNO, the British were benevolent in granting independence. Nonetheless, from its inception, UMNO had established the narration of being the protector of 'Bangsa Melayu' and the image developed along this dominant line. Under Dato' Onn and other Malay leaders such as Haji Anwar bin Abd. Malik, Haji Syed Alwi bin Syed Sheikh al-Hadi, Datuk Haji Abdul Wahab (Panglima Bukit Gantang) and Zainal Abidin Ahmad (Za'aba) (Abd. Samad 2011), a call for unity was made by the Malays nationwide instead of '*kerajaan*'.

The image and reputation of UMNO was enhanced because the leaders were able to build and uphold an image of sacrifice, commitment and dedication. They were perceived as sincere in their struggle to protect Malays from being politically and economically exploited and dominated by the immigrants. By taking these steps in the context of UMNO's constituents, the UMNO leadership presented the Malay position and was, thus, construed as the champion (*pejuang*) of the Malay community. The Malays joined UMNO because they wanted to be identified with a successful organisation that had motivated solidarity and group feeling. Thus, it became legitimate and rational to be identified with a group that is predominantly strong and acts for the same cause and goal. Over a short period of time, UMNO became the dominant force in Malaya's and later Malaysia's political environment. It was group feeling and unity emanating from the various nationalist movements throughout the Malay States, Strait Settlements and Singapore that provided the strength to achieve their collective interests. UMNO was effective in claiming and using the narrative of it being responsible for the collective good of the Malays for which party members and Malay masses owe their gratitude to UMNO. The many moves, initiatives and acts of UMNO established what I consider something akin to the Khaldunian notion of a 'tribe' (see Chapter 2).

UMNO portrayed the image that on certain principled issues, it was not willing to compromise where in fact it would take a pragmatic posture for the sake of coalition politics and expediency. According to Angelo Panebianco's (1988) theory, writing on political organisation, organisation has the tendency to desire retaining its formative behaviour (image), that is sticking to its original ideology when formed. This could be correct finding but not necessarily in all cases. Dato' Onn for example as a popular First President of UMNO could not change the party to be multi-ethnic despite the Party's Executive organ's endorsement. UMNO's general assembly and members refused to change the party ideology since the primary purpose at inception was for it to be a Malay movement. In this case, Pancbianco's theory proves to be right. Of course, had this happened, the political history and the politics of Malaya and Malaysia would have taken a different route. However, undeniably UMNO was truly a party capable of demonstrating its pragmatism when it wanted to prove itself as a political party. It was willing to make adjustments to its ideology of being a Malay party based on the dictate of the political environment. This challenge arose in the Municipal elections of February 1952. At that time, Dato' Onn, after he left UMNO, had already established his new multi-ethnic party Independent Malayan Party (IMP) and the party would contest the Municipal election of Kuala Lumpur as a non-communal party. UMNO, for its survival, had to counter and take action against the IMP's influence. This was the first serious challenge to UMNO as an ethnic party contesting in the town areas where the support of the non-Malay voters was critical. The men responsible for this ad hoc alliance were Yahya bin Dato' Abdul Rahman, the UMNO Kuala Lumpur Chairman of the election sub-committee and Colonel H. S. Lee an influential member of the Malayan Chinese Association (MCA). UMNO under Tunku Abdul Rahman negotiated and agreed to form an ad hoc alliance with MCA, an organisation founded in 1949 to contest the municipal election. It should be appreciated that it was a landmark decision for UMNO to compromise because both political parties were at opposite ends on the issue of citizenship. UMNO a party established in 1946, was opposed to granting citizenship on liberal terms to non-Malays, while MCA was adamantly for it.

Tunku's formula for political survival was for UMNO to contest the election as a Malayan party. He was willing and ready to make a first compromise with MCA though it was a departure from UMNO's original goal and ideology. This proved to be successful, opening the road to a more permanent political relationship in August 1953 and the formation of the *Perikatan* (National Alliance Organisation). In 1954, the coalition was joined by the Malayan Indian Congress (MIC). This was the beginning of UMNO's many compromises for political expediency. Thereafter, UMNO decided to realign its ideology of not only advancing the Malay rights but embracing the other races. According to Dr. Ismail bin Dato' Abdul Rahman, this was contrary to Tunku's original position (Ahmad Farouk 2002). UMNO's cooperation with the British allowed it to make a fundamental compromise though under the influence of the British colonial government who had promised to grant early independence if UMNO could live and work together with the other races.

UMNO under Tunku's leadership accepted the fact (though the position was influenced by the British) that it could not change the political realities of the country with the presence of large immigrant ethnic communities. How did UMNO cope with this new phenomenon? During this time, UMNO started to shift its focus from the 'systems of solidarity' to 'systems of interests' when it had to face the IMP in the municipal election of 1952. UMNO decided to work together with MCA in the election and succeeded in obtaining the majority seats, whereas IMP managed to win two seats only.

It was very clear from its infancy that leadership that was strong played a fundamental role on UMNO's group feeling and its behaviour. What should be the next step to be taken in its efforts to attain self-rule and independence? UMNO's leadership who in the majority were Malay aristocrats and elites understood the Malay political and cultural values and generally exploited its usefulness consistent with Ibn Khaldun's theory of leadership. Values such as *adab* (good manners), *santun* (courtesy) and *budibahasa* (appropriate language) and unwillingness to go against or to disagree openly with the leaders strengthened the party. It was the incentives of self-rule and independence that caused UMNO to change its *modus operandi* and adjust itself to be relevant to operate in a multi-racial Malayan environment. For the country to be independent, in the words of Lyttleton, Secretary of State in the Colonial Office, it must be inclusive of all ethnic communities. The British used pressure and inducement of 'Merdeka' as the desired position; various races in the country must live and work together (Funston 1980).

On the other hand, the colonial authority kept on insisting that immigrant workers' presence was temporary and, at the same time, they maintained close relationships and trust with the Sultans. For a long period, they did not encounter any difficulties as the leaderships remained intact, and the party members remained loyal and faithful. According to Silcock (1949: 455–456), "So long as Malaya remains politically unsophisticated and is firmly controlled by British administrators backed by British troops, it is possible to call it a Malay country and assume that Chinese and Indians are aliens without implying any intention to take any drastic action against them".

There was ample evidence of UMNO being constructively flexible in decision-making even on major or principled matters for political expediency. In 1951, before the election, the slogan *'Hidup Melayu'*, was changed to 'Merdeka' to accommodate the newly formed cooperation with the other races. In the Merdeka negotiation, there were many quiet bargains made and not mentioned in writing. One was an understanding then that the Malays would retain control over politics and government while the non-Malays be allowed to have a free hand in the economic and commercial spheres. The next part of this understanding was explicitly included in the Constitution.

This *quid pro quo* or what is referred to as the Social Contract, was that UMNO would protect the vital interests of the non-Malays in return for the non-Malays recognising the Malay rights that include the following: Bahasa Melayu is made the national language of the country, Islam is specified in the Constitution as the religion of the Federation but other religions would be allowed to be practised without interference and the non-Malays recognised the special positions of the Malays and the status of the Malay rulers. In return, the non-Malays gained a fundamental concession from UMNO on citizenship which was very liberal, particularly *jus soli* to those born after the Independence Day (after 31 August 1957).

In addition, citizenship was also granted with qualifications to any person whose father was a citizen at the time of his birth. According to Eric A. Nordlinger, very few other overseas Chinese in the other Southeast Asian countries could ever dream of getting such concessions (Nordlinger 1972). They were also given rights to take part in politics and government administration and unhindered participation in the economy and allowed religious freedom and liberal use of their languages for non-official purposes. This fundamental change was never referred to the party and Malay masses. Those who opposed felt why was there a need for a compromise and what was the need for 'Merdeka' to be secured in a hurry before sorting out important outstanding issues.

Nevertheless, it was pushed through by the leadership of UMNO. Yet, many considered this was not a tit for tat trade-off but the inherent birth rights of non-Malays. The Malays were not sure of the non-Malay's commitment and loyalty to

Malaya. However, it is important to note that UMNO's biggest compromise was against its own raison *d'étre* as it could damage its legitimacy and identity. UMNO was dependent on being seen as a Malay organisation but it moved away from being a Malay organisation to become a Malayan national entity. It is true to say that the dominant narration of the elite leadership allowed with the passage of time the organisational ideology to disappear and remain only as an ideal. The biggest compromise was already agreed.

## 3.3 Malay Solidarity *('asabiyyah)* and the Rise of UMNO

UMNO's peaceful struggle for independence, rejection of the British-proposed MU and the establishment of *Persekutuan Tanah Melayu* (lit. Federation of Malay Homelands but known as Federation of Malaya) on 1 February 1948 and ability to transfer *'kerajaan'* and *'Semangat Kenegerian'* (state spirit) to that of *'Semangat Kebangsaan'* (National Spirit) pacified the Malays and elevated UMNO's status and prestige among the Malays (Leetee 2007; Adib 2003; Cheah Boon Kheng 1988, 2007). UMNO also exhibited to the colonial authority that it was a moderate political party bent on championing the cause of the Malays. UMNO's slogan of 'Merdeka' symbolising unity and solidarity spoke of trustworthiness and a united front for independence of all races. In fact, UMNO delivered independence without shedding a single drop of blood. The image and branding of UMNO was successful to make other political players and stakeholders see it as a champion of their rights and freedom to the extent it was considered as a saviour of the Malays and Malaysia. UMNO lived up to the aspirations of the Malay community and, at the same time, it established a track record of practising politics of accommodation and compromise.

The Malay masses placed trust in the successive UMNO leaderships and agreed with the new approach and initiatives for cooperation. The Malays developed a growing confidence in UMNO's fight for retaining the status and dignity of the Malays and its philosophy of protecting race, religion and the nation. Malays perceive UMNO from its birth as a champion of the Malay community and Islamic values. This cemented the loyalty of the members to UMNO as being a reliable and trustworthy organisation, for which they must show gratitude. True to what Dato' Onn said: "UMNO *itu Melayu dan Melayu itu* UMNO" means 'UMNO are Malays and Malays are UMNO' and the two were synonymous and inseparable. This politics of identity allowed the participation of the community in the organisation, motivated by high degree of solidarity and common political ideology and social goals. UMNO and its leadership then were able to give identity, recognition and direction to the Malays and outline the ideology or set of shared values that served as the source of solidarity and unity.

This was evidenced in UMNO's ability to attract the Malays to participate in protests against British rule in a number of ways such as non-cooperation and wearing of mourning attire to show resistance and non-recognition of the colonial administration. UMNO's call for the non-recognition of the Governor-designate and for the

Sultan to abstain from attending any official functions involving the MU government was faithfully implemented. It was also UMNO that prompted Malay members of the Advisory Council of the Union not to attend the Council meeting. UMNO assumed the leadership role well and the British saw the resistance to be serious and effective, which made them withdraw the MU. The significance of the year 1946 was that it was a historical landmark that motivated the Malay spirit of Malayness. This '*Semangat 46*' spirit was what made UMNO and '*Hidup Melayu*' become the basic political philosophy of the Malay community, which led to the formation of UMNO and its eventual national hegemony across the country.

These acts and activities added value to the reputation and status of UMNO as the true defender/protector of the Malay community. The state and district level organisations were revived as a result of the resurgence of the Malay political and ethnic consciousness. It was inevitable, therefore, for UMNO to become the focal point of Malay political identity and ideology. It was able to subsequently play a dominant role in the coalition party as a leader and the strongest party in the coalition. Hence, UMNO attracted and maintained the overwhelming support of the Malays. The Malays during this time asked the most pertinent question of what separated them before and how they could work as '*Melayu Se Malaya*' (The Malay Congress of Malaya)? The 41 Malay associations, organisations and movements of divergent philosophical and ideological orientations throughout Malaya attended a national level 'Kongres' on 1–4 March 1946. They melted out their differences and resolved to unite under one political organisation, UMNO, for the sake of survival of the Malays. With this they possessed a common platform and shared values.

The British policy of forcing the Malays to accept the MU changed them from "having a very diverse and narrow state sentiment and viewpoints, seeing the reality confronting them, and rising up to oppose the British grand design" (see original text in Bahasa Malaysia in the footnote)[3] (Wan Teh 2017). They rose in a spontaneous manner and became united for a common cause to protect themselves against the communist threat posed by the Malayan Communist Party (MCP), who were mostly Chinese, to save their position and status in their own country. The Malays united to protect their race from being politically and economically overwhelmed by the immigrant ethnic minorities.

According to George Friedman (2018), "leaders of all sorts of political organizations emerge because they understand the historical moment and submit". In the game of politics like what Ibn Khaldun described in his political theory of '*asabiyyah*', it is necessary for the leader to establish group feeling and solidarity, in order to gain political power. UMNO would not be able to rise, unite the Malays, reinstate the position of the Malay rulers and abort the British grand design of MU without having wise leadership throughout its history. It was the pioneering spirit of the leaders of UMNO with their wisdom, charisma and integrity that seized the historical moment. The leaders of UMNO from 1946 up to the era of Tun Mahathir had the ability to assess the situation and make a decision on what is the best for the majority of the

---

[3] "*Berbagai sentimen kenegeriaan dan pemandangan yang sempit, sekarang mereka melihat realiti di depan mereka, telah bangkit menentang rancangan itu*".

people. All its successive leaders sincerely and honestly pursued 'prosper the Malays' first' policy without embezzlement of public funds and national wealth. They neither abused power nor misused public institutions and office for their parochial interests. They were willing to stand for what is right, even if it means resigning, such as the resignation of Dato' Onn Jaafar and Hussein Onn.

The leaders of UMNO then were perceived by the *rakyat* as leaders of integrity. They were not tainted with any allegations of abuse of power or misuse of public funds or public offices for their own personal vested interests. They neither abused power nor misused public institutions and office for their own personal vested interests. UMNO leaders early in its struggle were able to portray this trajectory of being the protector of the Malay race and were able to convince their supporters.

In connection with the image portrayed by the early leaders of UMNO, it cannot be denied that the birth of the nation resulted from the struggles of the sons of Malaya driven by Dato' Onn Jaafar who was able to get the trust of the Malay elites and masses. His leadership was instrumental in galvanising the Malay unity and solidarity to enable the establishment of UMNO. In the words of Tan Sri Mohamed Noordin Sopiee (2005), 'the Malays became a race awakened'. Dato' Onn was thus known as the "Initiator of Independence" ("Pengasas Kemerdekaan"). After failing in his attempts (twice) to convince his party, the UMNO, to open its doors to other races, i.e., a multi-ethnic party, he decided to resign and leave the party.

Upon leaving UMNO, Dato' Onn Jaafar established initially a multi-ethnic party under IMP and later Parti Negara Malaya (PNM), which was considered as an ultra-Malay party. In both instances, he failed to convince the Malays or garner the support of the *rakyat* for his ideals. It is interesting to note that even with a big name like his, the Malays were already entrenched with UMNO that he started and were not willing to change loyalty.

The success of UMNO in garnering the overwhelming support of the Malays, which led to Malaya achieving its independence and later on the formation of Malaysia was closely tied to the characters and personalities of its leaders. Tunku Abdul Rahman (the Tunku) took over from Dato' Onn. It was a clever move by UMNO leadership then to invite Tunku to lead UMNO as he was a close member of the Malay ruler in the state of Kedah. He made the negotiations with the Malay monarchy and the British in making independence easier.

In fact, when the British engineered the politics of compromise, UMNO under Tunku agreed to the formula which expedited the gaining of independence. He was trusted by the colonial power, the Malay rulers and the non-Malays. Malaysia gained independence on 31 August 1957 and he was rightly considered as the "Father of Independence". In 1969, after the racial riots, Tunku was blamed and forced to resign. He was replaced by Tun Abdul Razak Hussein, who was his deputy. UMNO yet again chose an aristocrat to succeed the Tunku.

Tun Razak was an able administrator, diplomat and negotiator. According to Sultan Nazrin Shah in his speech at the launch of the book "*Fulfilling a Legacy*", he "was a man of honour and dignity, who not only fulfilled his duties sincerely but also dedicated the final hours of his life to the country".[4] In fact, some people in UMNO

---

[4] For original text, refer to archive https://sultannazrinshah.com/category/2017-speeches/page/2/.

leaderships' circle would consider Tun Razak as the mover of the country in Tunku's administration. He was called "Bapa Pembangunan" ("Father of Development"). He played a very effective role in the separation of Singapore and negotiations for ending the confrontation with Indonesia, and he was the architect in the introduction of the NEP domestically. It was during his premiership that UMNO was beginning to experience factionalism and disunity especially with the slogan of Tun Razak replacing the "Old Order" of UMNO with the "New Order", which caused a lot of discomfort within the old guards of UMNO. His choice of his own brother-in-law (Tun Hussein Onn) as the DPM with the sudden death of Tun Dr. Ismail also created a rift within UMNO and Ghafar Baba the most senior of the vice presidents of UMNO refused to accept any position in the government. With the unexpected death of Tun Razak in London, Tun Hussein Onn succeeded him. He was not only well educated but also considered a principled and a man of high integrity. These factors coupled with the fact that they were all from noble or aristocratic families endeared them to the Malays and they were all held in high regard. This, directly or indirectly, reflected the Malay psyche prevalent during the period.

Be that as it may, in the mid-1970s, UMNO was a divided party. The situation was further aggravated with the charges brought against Dato' Harun Idris, a charismatic and popular Chief Minister of Selangor for corruption. This caused disunity within UMNO. Tun Hussein Onn also faced difficulty in his choice of DPM, as he wanted to choose someone he could comfortably work with and not from among the party vice presidents as was traditionally and conventionally the case. He made the decision to appoint Tun Mahathir after a long gap after receiving a warning that if he were to choose outside the party hierarchy of the vice presidents, they would all resign. At this time, he could not take the risk. After five years of leading UMNO and the government, he decided to resign citing health reasons but the truth of the matter was that there were a lot of backbiting and unsavoury political intrigues that made him go.

When Tun Mahathir succeeded Tun Hussein as PM in 1981 in the UMNO-led government, he somewhat broke this pattern of the Malay elites ruling the country. He had the reputation of being a radical and a reformist when Tun Razak first brought him to the Cabinet. He was stamped as an ultra-Malay nationalist. His style of leadership and policies changed Malaysia from an agro-based country to an industrialised nation. He placed Malaysia on the map of the world by taking high profile foreign policy initiatives and postures. He synchronised Peninsular Malaysia time with Sabah and Sarawak. In order to overcome corruption and money politics, he introduced the motto 'Clean, Efficient and Trustworthy' ('*Bersih, Cekap dan Amanah*') when he was first appointed as PM. This reflected his focus and determination in rendering services to the people with integrity. On this, he did not succeed. Interestingly, he introduced the same policy and motto under the PH as the Seventh PM.

Malaysia's success story happened in the 22 years of his premiership and his return to power in 2018 that brought down the BN-led government whose leaders were tainted by financial scandals, corruptions and abuse of power clearly demonstrates his charisma and leadership character of high moral integrity. The success of the

political party, *'asabiyyah* and *'umran* depend very much on the leadership. UMNO
fell from grace because of 'leadership' and PH came to power because of 'leadership'.

## 3.4  UMNO's Achievements: Towards *'umranic* State

How do we measure UMNO's achievements and what would be the right yardstick
to use? Would it be accurate to say the success of government policies led and dominated by UMNO should be considered as UMNO's achievements? A political party
upholds certain principles regarding public policies of the government, seeks to attain
and maintain political power within the government. So, political parties can play
essential roles such as opinion making, acting as a watchdog introducing candidates,
bridge between government and people, and proposed useful political programmes.
They bring people together to control the government, develop policies favourable
to their interests or the groups that support them, and organise and persuade voters to
elect their candidates to office. For the purpose of this study, it is, therefore, safe to
apply the achievements of the government as that of the party controlling the government. The achievements of the government are also that of UMNO because firstly
UMNO led the country, secondly UMNO was the dominant party in the coalition
and finally the President of UMNO was also the PM of the country. Therefore, it is
fair to assume in a parliamentary system, the achievements of the government should
be considered as the success of the ruling political party. In this regard, government
and UMNO will be referred to interchangeably.

UMNO's achievements were of two types: (1) political and (2) economic development. Malaya/Malaysia was viewed as the most successful example of a multi-
racial state upon its independence on 31 August 1957 (Ozey 1988). The indigenous
Malays, Chinese and Indians had all agreed upon independence to be part of the
nation premised on a compromise and politics of accommodation. Today, Malaysia
can be considered as one of the most successful Asian nations and one able to have
effectively transited into a modern economy. Therefore, it can be said that the success
can be attributed to UMNO's leadership of the government under the Alliance and
BN, respectively. Thus, the party had won 13 successive GEs to govern Malaysia
since independence in 1957. The rise of UMNO from the 1940s should be understood
from this perspective. After such a sterling record of achievements, its performance
began to slide drastically from the 12th and 13th GEs in 2008 and 2013, respectively.
This was a clear indication of changing political and cultural values towards empha-
sising on people's rights and democracy and how eventually UMNO lost peoples'
mandate in the May 2018 GE (the decline of UMNO is discussed in Chapter 4).

Since independence in 1957, Malaysia has grown tremendously to become a
more developed country over six decades. Politically, the three ethnic communities
agreed to work together in a coalition of three main ethnic-based political parties
namely the Malays under the UMNO, ethnic Chinese under MCA and the ethnic
Indians subsequently joined under the Malaysian Indian Congress (MIC). These
main ethnic political parties formed the Alliance and became the pioneer political

party of the new multi-ethnic nation with each retaining its separate ethnic identity. It can be said that each community evolved its own solidarity or '*asabiyyah* at times without interference from other ethnic communities but through socialisation and cooperation, they collaborated for political expediency.

This was a unique compromise and sacrifice in the political history of a country and the world, where total aliens were granted automatic citizenship by the stroke of a pen. The researcher agrees with Ronald Cecil Hamlyn McKie (1963) in his memoir when he described that there was no pressure to make non-Malays and non-Muslims Malayan/Malaysian. In his view, Malaysian is not a national, or a racial term and it does not refer to any religious belief. Against this unfavourable backdrop, each race is allowed to maintain and perpetuate its own identity without feeling Malaysian psychologically, emotionally, culturally, economically, politically and socially without any restrictions and limitations. Malaya became a multi-racial flexible country without specific direction or any form of imposition of national identity (McKie 1963).

Moreover, at the end of the Japanese occupation and their surrender, during the transition and before the British Military Administration took over, the Malay community was facing brutal atrocities at the hands of the mainly ethnic Chinese guerrilla group, the Malayan People's Anti-Japanese Army (MPAJA). For a short term of 14 days during the MPAJA rule, the Malays suffered brutal acts of violence. It would be fully justified to say that the Japanese occupation and the MU introduction acted as catalysts for the fast-changing Malay political attitude on the subjects of the Sultan and state loyalty and allegiance known as '*semangat kenegerian*' (Awang 1983).

In its rhetoric, UMNO repeatedly said it was the party that saved the Sultans and the *rakyat*. UMNO took up the Malay cause and successfully organised protests against the MU proposal with the strong support by the Malay media and teachers associations. The media brought the Malay issues to the centre and helped to inflame Malays against the MU. UMNO became the true champion of the Malay cause to protect the special status of the Malay community and the Sultans. The newfound group feeling of the Malays, sense of togetherness and shared political destiny and future expressed in '*Semangat Kebangsaan*' (National Spirit) germinated the seeds for the formation of UMNO, which was followed through by its institutionalisation. This sense of nationalism made them realise that they have a strong common bond culturally and socially.

It can be said that the Johore Malay Association (*Persatuan Melayu Johor*) led by English-educated Malays in the government service was the precursor to the revival of Malay organisations. These were social organisations whose principal objective was the protection of the Malay privileges *vis-à-vis* the new plan of the government. The most notable of these organisations was the Peninsular Malay Movement of Johore (*Pergerakan Melayu Semenanjung Johor* [PMSJ]). UMNO became a political party that shaped the Malaysian political landscape and remained in power for almost 61 years, definitely making it one of the longest in the world.

The Malays have not been revolutionary or radical in their initiatives or approaches on their grievances or discontent. However, for the first time in December 1945, they organised a public demonstration to condemn the MU Plan. When MacMichael arrived in Kota Bahru, an estimated crowd of 10,000 confronted him. Among the placards they displayed was: "Malaya belongs to the Malays. We don't want the other races to be given the rights and privileges of the Malays". If prior to these, protests were carried out by the elites, on this occasion the anti-MU movements saw participation by every segment of the Malay community. The withdrawal of the MU on 31 January 1948 by the British without the Malays resorting to any form of violence, reinstating the position and status of the Sultans from dissolution to become relevant was a laudable example in the annals in the history of the struggle for independence of Malaya (Abd. Samad 2011). UMNO continued to play a fundamental role in pre- and post-independence Malaya and in 1963 in the formation of Malaysia with Sabah, Sarawak and Singapore.

UMNO, as the ruling political party in government, saved Malaysia from being a failed state as predicted by a British Secretary Allen Lennox Boyd for the Commonwealth and Overseas Territories in Parliament (Datar 1983), by adopting an inclusive policy for all races. By the social contract of 1957, more than a million migrants became citizens overnight without the necessity of showing loyalty and associations with the country socially or culturally. This is a landmark in the history of immigration in the world. The Malays, in fact, sacrificed from being a *bangsa* (nation) to the *kaum* (ethnic group) by that policy decision. That is considered a pristine example of inclusiveness.[5] Upon achieving its success, it made the single biggest political compromise, to be inclusive of others in Malaya, by granting citizenship. Due to this courageous decision, UMNO was able to convince the British colonial government that UMNO can lead the country to independence through self-rule by working with the Chinese and Indians and not going alone. This was the start of the power sharing political module among the major races in Malaysia. Tunku Abdul Rahman's name entered the first page of 'Encyclopaedia of Democracy' because of this Social Contract. Everyone would like to talk about one's achievements and UMNO is no different. In more than six decades of its existence, it cannot be denied that it had contributed significantly and tremendously to the country's political and economic developments as well as growth in all dimensions. Its track record speaks for itself from 1957 with the attainment of the country's independence; it continued with its nation building programmes with an unparalleled record of success.

From 1957 to 1970, UMNO was at the forefront of the country's political developments. It was pro-active in building a divided nation of multi-ethnic, multi-cultural and multi-religious diversity into a harmonious, peaceful and politically stable nation. UMNO was seen by its members, the Malays and other citizens, as a political party that never stood on the sidelines of history or acted as a mere observer. It planned and crafted policies to bring justice, unity and economic developments to all its citizens even though it was a party formed for the Malays. It was the party that brought independence and gave its multi-ethnic population citizenship, accepted power sharing political compromise and equality of all citizens before the law in a social contract that

---

[5] Direct communication with Dr. Rais Saniman, scholar and co-author of the book *Growth and Ethnic Inequality* on the NEP on 3 March 2019 (Faaland et al. 1990).

benefitted all. When the emergency due to communist insurgencies was brought to an end in the country's first decade of independence, UMNO being the leading party launched a policy against poverty Malaya had inherited from the colonial administration and opened up new land settlement areas under Federal Land Development Authority (FELDA) scheme to give land to the landless to earn a living and brought development to the urban areas to make the country flourish and prosper.

After 12 years of the Alliance's rule, economic development and growth was achieved but the country witnessed a disproportionate pattern of wealth distribution in which the Chinese held the big proportion of the wealth as compared to the other two main ethnic groups in the country. Poverty was largely prevalent among the Malays and Indians since the Malays lived in the rural areas and the Indians in the estates, whereas the Chinese were mainly in urban locations of the country. This situation reflected the differences in the incidence of poverty particularly in Peninsular Malaysia. The household monthly income of 1970 in the Peninsular ranged from as low as RM276 for the Malays, followed by RM478 for the Indians and RM632 for the Chinese. According to Abdul Hakim Roslan (2001) and Erik Thorbeckc and Chutatong Charumilind (2002), the unequal distribution of wealth among ethnic groups created ethnic tension in the Malaysian society. During the 1960s, there was increased ethnic polarisation especially in the GE of 1969. In that election, the campaign atmosphere was tense and heated with a lot of racial undertones along sensitive issues including the demand for racial equality at all levels of political, social economic, cultural and educational activities.

In the instant context, is it possible for a country like Malaysia to suggest the hegemony of one community to be abolished? Based on the historical background of the nation, its racial composition and diversity, it is still not possible just to do away with the affirmative policies as they are necessary to narrow the economic gaps between ethnic groups. It is argued that the component of the Alliance especially the MCA suffered a devastating defeat at the hands of the Democratic Action Party (DAP) due to this policy, while UMNO remained strong and intact. The DAP playing its ethnic Chinese card attracted the Chinese voters in the urban areas, who had given their strong support to the DAP as the voice of the Chinese. They gained more state seats in Penang, Selangor and Perak with Chinese majority voters, who opposed the Alliance. The votes reflected the sentiments of the Chinese against the government led by the Malays or UMNO. Unfortunately, victory celebration organised by the DAP and GERAKAN in Kuala Lumpur on 13 May 1969 went overboard by namecalling and insulting words and placards against the Malays. It must be noted that DAP was a newly rebranded political party after the separation of Singapore from Malaysia. DAP is a successor party of the People Action Party (PAP) of Singapore, that had used ethnic sentiments of the Chinese when they were part of Malaysia.

For the first time in the history of Malaysia, racial conflicts and riots sprouted on 13 May 1969 in states with huge Chinese population, i.e., Selangor, Penang and Perak. Law and order could not be restored, and emergency was declared and Parliament was suspended. The military took over the country but held power for a short period just to establish law and order and decided to hand over the country back to the civilian authority. Under the Emergency Ordinance, the National Operations

Council (NOC) was set up to tackle the new crisis. Tunku was heavily criticised by UMNO members as the PM of Malaysia for failing to solve the economic disparities and gap between the Malays and other races. In 1970, Tunku decided to resign and handed the helm of power to his Deputy, Tun Razak, who became the Director of Operations of the NOC.

Tun Razak became the Second PM of Malaysia on 22 September 1970 until January 1976, when he succumbed to cancer. To the credit of UMNO, it was its leadership under Tun Razak that brought back parliamentary democracy to the country after he restored law and order. Tun Razak after the 13 May 1969 tragedy, decided the country should focus on economic development, whereby leadership of the government led by UMNO quickly acted to identify the root causes of the racial conflict. UMNO then reviewed new approaches to its economic, political and cultural policies. It introduced the NEP in 1970, as a principal policy in response to the conflict. The NEP was a social engineering policy to restructure the Malaysian society so that the citizens would not be identified through their economic function and to eradicate poverty irrespective of race. It was the first of its kind in the world with the aim of creating a more just and equitable society where every Malaysian can benefit. This policy targeted not economic growth per se but growth with equity where no one group would feel marginalised. At the same time, it also introduced another arm of the policy that is the eradication of poverty irrespective of race. It was through the NEP that the country was to regain peace and stability as well as economic growth. This resulted in its ability to produce great numbers of Malay professionals and entrepreneurs. The NEP played a vital role in the history of politics and economy of Malaysia. Malaysia achieved the reduction of poverty as well as the creation of a Malay middle and business classes in the society. Other than achieving the NEP objectives, it brought various consequences which proved to be beneficial to the well-being of the country and people as a whole.

Without UMNO, the Malays would still be left far behind in business, educational and employment opportunities due to historical injustices committed during the colonial period. In fact, due to these reasons, UMNO was construed as the saviour of the Malays except for the last decade of the 61-year rule. UMNO's policy and the engendering of the Malay middle class resulted in the creation of one of the foundations of Malaysia's economic growth for the last three decades. In the post-1969 era, UMNO played a bigger role and dictated government policies but was strongly supported by the Malays. Tun Razak even said that: "the government is a government which is shouldered by UMNO, and to UMNO I hand the responsibility of determining the pattern of government that will emerge" (Ah-Bang 1975: 90). These firm and assertive words of Tun Razak was translated into policies which accelerated expansion of *bumiputera* (son of the soil) middle class, capital accumulation through government intervention and the creation of Malay capitalists. In the 1970s, the government was able to lead and build comprehensive systems and institutions to help the Malay participations, such as Bank Bumiputera Malaysia (1965), the Urban Development Authority (UDA), *Perbadanan Nasional* (PERNAS), Bank Pembangunan and State Economic Development Corporations. These systems and institutions helped create Malay capitalists and entrepreneurs. More universities were established like Universiti Kebangsaan Malaysia (UKM); Institut Teknologi MARA (ITM), known as Universiti Teknologi MARA (UiTM) now; and much later International Islamic University Malaysia (IIUM) on 23 May 1983; and quotas were also introduced to admit *Bumiputeras* into the Universities. Maktab Rendah Sains MARA (MRSM) or Junior Science College MARA and many other institutions and agencies were created to open up education opportunities to *Bumiputeras*. The government gave scholarships and easy term loans to help Malays to catch up and to produce more academics and professionals. These were very effective social restructuring programmes that benefitted the Malays and other ethnic communities tremendously.

UMNO has contributed tremendously in the development of the nation and the *rakyat*. The monumental achievement of UMNO does not come in a vacuum because it is viewed as successful in carrying out the aspirations of the masses in cohesive unity; and brought shared prosperity to change the lifestyles of the people. It was UMNO that brought a new approach by uniting the Malay nationalist movements to be formed under one wing of political awareness called UMNO and introduced coalition politics. Upon achieving its success, it made the single biggest political compromise to be inclusive of the others in Malaya through granting of citizenship. Due to this courageous decision, UMNO was able to convince the British colonial government that it could lead the country to independence beginning with self-rule working with the Chinese and Indians and not doing it alone. It must be remembered that it could have decided to go alone and this was the start of the politics of coalition or power sharing model among the major races. This was the formula applied from the time of the First PM, Tunku Abdul Rahman, followed by Tun Abdul Razak, Tun Hussein Onn, Tun Dr. Mahathir Mohammad, Tun Abdullah Badawi and Dato' Seri Najib Tun Abdul Razak as the last PM from UMNO. UMNO's history was one of sacrifices with the hope of bringing greater good to fulfil the aspirations of the people of all walks of life. It was believed and trusted by the multi-ethnic community and gave UMNO the mandate for 60 years.

From 1981 to 1990, when the nation faced an economic crisis and recession, it was UMNO/BN government that implemented the new policy of industrialisation to overcome the crisis. UMNO, as the dominant party of the coalition BN government, implemented broad-ranging infrastructure development policies to accelerate economic growth as well as modernise the economy. From Tun Mahathir's economic success of modernising Malaysia to Tun Abdullah Ahmad Badawi when he came to power in 2003 and finally Najib in 2009, the leaders have always played a fundamental role in bringing progress and prosperity to the country ensuring at all times that they fulfilled peoples' aspirations for a better life, prosperity, trustworthiness and that they can be trusted to work by the people. But the symptoms of the slide downwards due to multiple reasons can be seen from the results of the 2008, 2013 and 2018 GEs. In any democratic system, the *rakyat* are the final arbiter on whether the political parties and its leaders had performed or not in accordance with their expectations and aspirations. When they were considered to have failed to deliver and there was public distrust, the consequences would be translated in the election results as were evident in 2004, 2008, 2013 and 2018 GEs. Moreover, from the perspectives of politics and economy, even though there was peace and stability as the country has reached an *'umrani* phase, the weakening of *'asabiyyah* due to lack of unity and solidarity, the lack of governance and corruption will cause a regime change as happened in GE14 in 2018, which is the focus of Chapter 4.

## 3.5 Conclusion

This chapter discusses the history of UMNO's establishment, its rise and ability to form the Malay *'asabiyyah* and UMNO's achievements towards creation of *'umranic* state. It discusses UMNO's evolution to prominence and political dominance. It was a catalyst for the growth of patriotism/nationalism and transforming the Malays' parochial state-centric outlook into a Pan-Malayan national consciousness. Originally, championing the Malay rights and freedoms against the British colonial rule, UMNO showed pragmatism and resilience and ability to transform the post-independent nation into one of the world's peaceful and harmonious developing state. UMNO's major compromise initiative was its policy of social contract, which granted citizenship to non-Malay Chinese and Indian ethnic minorities brought by Britain when it administered Malaya.

Even though UMNO could rule the country alone, in line with its policy of accommodation, it ruled the country for six decades in coalition with its Chinese and Indian ethnic coalition partners. UMNO's success is attributed to its wise and sincere leadership committed to the cause of Malay rights and freedom within the frame work of Malayan Federation. UMNO leaders played a fundamental role in shaping the political landscape of the country from colonial time to independence. They were able to form solidarity and unity among the Malays and accommodate the immigrant ethnic groups into the body politic of the country. UMNO's inclusive policy changed and uplifted lives of all Malaysians.

## References


Abd. Samad P (2011) The myth of Dato' Onn Jaafar: the forgotten hero: reinventing history. Partisan Publication and Distribution, Kuala Lumpur

Abdul Wahid ZA (1977) Semangat Perjuangan Melayu. Jebat: Malaysian. J Hist Polit Strat Stud 07–08:1–9

Adib M (2003) Reflections of free independence Malaya. Pelanduk Publications, Kuala Lumpur

Ah-Bang L (1975) New directions in Malaysia. In: Institute of Southeast Asian Studies (ed) Southeast Asian affairs 1975. Jurong: FEP International Ltd, pp 87–97

Ahmad Farouk AF (2002) Culture and politics: an analysis of United Malays National Organisation (UMNO) 1946–1999. Master's thesis, Universiti Malaya, Kuala Lumpur

Awang Z (1983) Coalition politics in Malaysia. Master's thesis, Western Michigan University. Scholarworks@WMU. https://scholarworks.wmich.edu/cgi/viewcontent.cgi?article=2579&context=masters_theses

Cheah Boon Kheng (1979) The Malayan Democratic Union 1945–1948. Master's thesis, Universiti Malaya, Kuala Lumpur

Cheah Boon Kheng (1988) The erosion of ideological hegemony and royal power and the rise of postwar Malay nationalism 1945–46. J Southeast Asian Stud 19(1):1–26

Cheah Boon Kheng (2007) New perspectives & research on Malaysian history. Malaysian Branch of the Royal Asiatic Society, Kuala Lumpur

Datar KK (1983) Quest for politics of consensus. Vikos, New Delhi

Faaland J, Parkinson JR, Saniman RB (1990) Growth and ethnic inequality. Malaysi''s new economic policy. Kuala Lumpur: Dewan Bahasa dan Pustaka

Funston J (1980) Malay politics in Malaysia: a study of the United Malays National Organisation and Parti Islam. Heinemann Asia, Kuala Lumpur

Friedman G (2018) The role of political leaders. Geopolitical Future. https://geopoliticalfutures.com/role-political-leaders/

Gungwu W (1981) Malayan nationalism. Community and nation: essays on Southeast Asia and the Chinese. Heinemann Educational Books, Kuala Lumpur

Khoon TC (1985) Malaysia today. Pelanduk Publications, Kuala Lumpur

Leetee R (2007) From Kampung to Twin Towers. Oxford Fajar, Kuala Lumpur

Mauzy DK (1982) Barisan Nasional: Coalition government in Malaysia. Marican, Kuala Lumpur

McKie RCH (1963) The emergence of Malaysia. Greenwood Press, Westport, CT

Miller H (1965) The story of Malaysia. Faber & Faber, London

Mohd. Basri AF (1992) The United Malays National Organization (UMNO) 1981–1991: a study of the mechanics of a changing political culture. PhD thesis, University of Hull

Nordlinger EA (1972) Conflict regulation in divided societies. Harvard University Press, Cambridge, MA

Omar A (1999) Malaya/Malaysia: state, nation, nationality, the emergence of nationhood in a vacuum. Paper Presented at a Conference on "Concepts of State, Identity and Nationhood in Southeast Asia", at the National University of Singapore, Kent Ridge, Singapore, 8–11 December 1999

Ozey M (1988) Development in Malaysia: poverty, wealth and trusteeship. INSAN, Kuala Lumpur

Panebianco A (1988) Political parties: organization and power. Cambridge University Press, Cambridge

Purcell V (1948) The Chinese in Malaya. Oxford University Press, London

Roff WR (1967) The origins of Malay nationalism. Yale University Press, New Haven, CT

Roslan AH (2001) Income inequality, poverty and development policy in Malaysia. School of Economics, Universiti Utara Malaysia, Kedah. https://www.semanticscholar.org/paper/Income-Inequality-%2C-Poverty-and-Development-Policy-Roslan/b93d23e72af6e595f549648315f7234ea3bba61c

Silcock TH (1949) Forces for unity in Malaya: observations of a European resident. Int Aff 25(4):453–465. https://doi.org/10.2307/3018421

Sopiee MN (2005) From Malayan Union to Singapore separation: political unification in the Malaysia region, 1945–1965. University Malaya Press, Kuala Lumpur

Stockwell AJ (1979) British policy and Malay politics during the Malayan Union experiment 1945–1948. MBRAS, Kuala Lumpur

Thorbecke E, Charumilind C (2002) Economic inequality and its socioeconomic impact. World Dev 30(9):1477–1495

Wan Ahmed SS (2010) Culture, power and resistance: post-colonialism, autobiography and Malaysian independence. PhD thesis, School of Applied Social Sciences, Durham University

Wan Teh WH (2017) Fasa Pertama Perjuangan UMNO Penuh Berani. Utusan Malaysia (UM), 11 May. https://wajabangsa.blogspot.com/2017/05/fasa-pertama-perjuangan-umno-penuh.html. Accessed on 1 August 2022

Winstedt R (1948) Malaya and its history. Hutchinson's University Library, London

# Chapter 4
# UNMO's Collapse of the Malay *'asabiyyah*

**Abstract** This chapter examines the factors leading to the erosion and decline of UMNO's power. After winning a record 13 successive elections, UMNO was probably one of the most successful political parties in the world. Bridget Welsh (2018) calls it the world's longest ruling political party. However, UMNO's six-decade rule came to an abrupt end on 9 May 2018 after Malaysia's 14th General Election. How can UMNO's decline be explained? Were there early indications of the weakening of the Malay *'asabiyyah* and UMNO's downfall? Why did UMNO leaders not foresee the possible outcome of the GE14?

**Keywords** Coalition · UMNO leaders · GE · Decline · The Malay *'asabiyyah*

## 4.1 Introduction

UMNO was one of the strongest political parties in the world and had won a record 13 successive elections. *The Malaysian Insight* on 1 June 2018 reported that outside of the communist system, UMNO was probably one of the most successful political parties in the world. Bridget Welsh (2018b) calls it the world's longest ruling political party. But on 9 May 2018 in Malaysia's GE14, UMNO's six-decade rule came to an abrupt end. Perceived as impossible by political observers, pollsters and political experts, UMNO prepared for handing over power to the newly formed anti-UMNO coalition of PH. How can UMNO's decline be explained? Were there early indications of the weakening of the Malay *'asabiyyah* and UMNO's downfall? Why did the leaders of UMNO not foresee the possible outcome of the GE14? This chapter discusses the factors of the decline of UMNO and its downfall on 9 May 2018.



S. H. bin Syed Jaafar Albar, *Ibn Khaldun's Theory and the Party-Political Edifice of the United Malays National Organisation*, SpringerBriefs in Political Science, https://doi.org/10.1007/978-981-19-7388-8_4

## 4.2  The Symptoms of UMNO's Decline

Symptom of a decline in the context of a political party is interpreted as the organisation being confronted with problems affecting its well-being. The main symptom of UMNO's decline was loss of voters' support towards the party and its leaders at both local (states) and parliamentary (national) levels evidenced in GE12 and GE13 held in 2008 and 2013, respectively. Therefore, first indicators of voters' support are discussed. Second, the results of GE12, GE13 and GE14 are analysed. Third, the issues of opportunities, strengths, threats and weaknesses of UMNO in the changing environment of Malay political culture are discussed.

Syed Arabi and Safar (1986), Baharudin Ali Masrom (1989), Mohd. Basri (1992) and Ahmad Atory Hussain (1998) all as cited in Kassim (2006) have argued that determinants of the voters' support towards UMNO included the quality of the candidate, the credibility and trustworthiness of the leadership, the party programmes organised at the grassroots level, the public image and perception especially of the leaders,[1] candidates'/leaders' propagation of ideas on different subjects such as economics, politics, democracy, freedom, the leaders'/candidates' involvements in governance and corruption, candidates engagement and friendliness with the electorates before and after the election, and finally, the candidate's/leadership's ability to influence or sway voters before and during the campaign periods.

Studies before these elections have shown that the determinant factors mentioned above have a strong correlation with the degree of voter support towards UMNO prior and during the elections. The decline of a political party voters' support, especially for a well-established party like UMNO, which held power since the independence of 1957, normally is a process and has a recognisable pattern or trend and it does not happen at the spur of the moment. Moreover, UMNO has a well-established network and organisational structure to chart out its activities. In order to evaluate the support towards UMNO, from the increase or decline perspective, it is fundamental to examine its historical roots starting with its past elections.

This method can be used against current performances and observations or forecasts on probable outcomes that can be made. For instance, data and records of UMNO election results, from 1978, 1982, 1986, 1990, 1999 and 2004, can be used against the outcomes of 2008, 2013 and 2018, and all are available for comparative purposes. In elections before 2008, UMNO performed exceptionally well by obtaining large majorities in terms of popular votes, at both the parliamentary and state levels, and in the elections of 2008, 2013 and 2018, results showed a marked reduction on popular votes and number of seats at the parliamentary and state levels. These are strong empirical evidences that point out to the decline of voters' support for UMNO. The movement in voter support from election to election (1959–2018) is clearly shown in Figs. 4.1 and 4.2 below.

---

[1] The public had negative perception about Tun Abdullah Badawi the 5th PM and Dato' Seri Najib Tun Abdul Razak, the 6th PM of Malaysia before the 2008 and 2013 General Elections, which affected the election results.

**Fig. 4.1**  Popular votes gained by BN during 1959–2018 (*Source* Today, 2018)

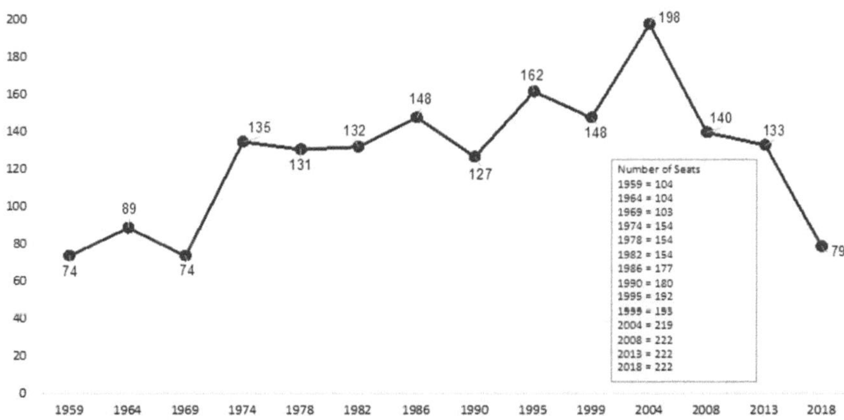

**Fig. 4.2**  Election Commission's Reports on General Elections from 1959 to 2018 (*Source* Today, 2018)

Figures 4.1 and 4.2 clearly demonstrate the ups and downs of UMNO's voters' support and number of seats, especially in the GEs of 2008 and 2013. It shows a reduction in popular votes and total number of seats at both state and parliamentary levels as well as the loss of two-thirds majority.

Some political analysts such as John Funston (2018), Clive Kessler (2018) and William Case (2010) argue that these outcomes are not the true position of voters' preference as they were achieved because the party had tight control over the government machineries and agencies, coupled with extensive funding at its disposal to be disbursed by the party machinery. Equally significant is the fact that the party's machinery and organisational structures are efficient. Hence, it was difficult to imagine how UMNO could be defeated in any election. In sum, it would be a challenge for any opposition party to match UMNO's financial and material resources. On the other hand, it is also true to say that the leadership and government policy initiatives had benefitted the *rakyat*; thus, the electorate had confidence in the leaders.

Underscored by these advantages and strengths, party leaders and grassroots went to the polls with the confidence that it would secure victory without any difficulty. Having achieved victory in previous elections allowed the outcome to be predictable, but the disadvantage was that the party developed a sense of complacency, over-confidence and took things for granted. They supposed that they knew before the elections what voters' sentiments were and what type of grassroots support could be expected. Usually, the forecasts on the possible outcomes would always be fairly accurate. Under the circumstances, it could be that the party at this time had ignored or did not bother to examine the voters' sentiments and available information to indicate the change of voters' preferences. In fact, the results of GE12 in 2008 and GE13 in 2013 (refer to Figs. 4.1 and 4.2) were evident of a swing of Malay and non-Malay voters, especially among the young, urban and lower- and upper-middle-class electorate across all ethnicities against the government.

These symptoms and factors exhibited voters' dissatisfactions and disillusionment with the leaderships and government policies and initiatives that were not responsive to the economic plight, problems and challenges faced by the *rakyat*. Naturally, these were manifested in the erosion of popular votes and parliamentary and state seats. The party's top leadership could have easily seen and anticipated which way the votes were going in 2018 if they had reflected on the election results of 2008 and 2013 and valued the sentiments expressed thereto. In retrospect, they were aware of the decline of support; however, they failed to take remedial action to correct the shortcomings and weaknesses. The party proceeded campaigning on the basis of business as usual, did not pay attention to the warning on matters not being as usual and that UMNO party supporters and grassroots have changed.[2]

The loss of the 2018 elections was an utter shock to UMNO leaders and everyone in the country, though the indicative signs of defeat existed prior to the elections. This researcher's own survey of UMNO leaders at branch, division and national levels prior to the election indicated that the majority agreed the mood for the 2018 election was against the incumbent government. In fact, the symptoms of election problems were already reflected in the 2008 and 2013 election results. The majority of the people whom the researcher spoke to admitted the probability of losing the election.

Unfortunately, the party leadership, being the incumbent and in control of the government and its machineries, categorised it as difficult yet deemed they would pull through in the election. None of the UMNO members at the grassroots and Supreme Council as well as Cabinet ministers believed they could lose the election.

---

[2] In the 2018 GE, the President of MCA and President of MIC lost their seats in constituencies that were BN's strongholds. In Johor, an incumbent Deputy Minister lost his seat in Muar to a newcomer Syed Saddiq and, in Johor Bharu, a senior UMNO politician and former Minister lost his seat to also a young newcomer from PH. Due to factionalism and not being known as a Najib man, the researcher was dropped from contesting the Kota Tinggi seat even though he always obtained the highest popular vote in the general elections.

Strangely, many of the fundamental issues that determined voters' sentiments were set aside or ignored. Although beginning from 2008 to 2013 and more evident in 2018, the signs were that the UMNO coalition would lose the election.

Many issues inundating UMNO especially on its leadership that came whether directly or indirectly from multiple sources remained outstanding and unanswered. Many UMNO insiders had predicted that they might lose the election but somehow they were miraculously hopeful that they would still pull through with a reduced majority. This was the state of mind-set during GE 2018.

UMNO and its coalition partners in the BN, formerly known as the Alliance until 1974, had been the dominant party for the last six decades. Malaysian politics has been very ethnic-centred since the time of independence in 1957; thus, UMNO as a Malay party utilised the winning formula for the elections to gain mass support from the Malay majority community and the government institutions that are generally inclined to support the party. This was the condition and state of affairs that safe-guarded the Malay political power. With development and progress, the society and nation began to witness and experience change, especially in the 1980s and 1990s.

In addition, there were disunity and factionalism brewing in UMNO. The group feeling and unity once enjoyed among the Malay society did not remain intact, and there was disintegration through development, urbanisation, factionalism and warlordism within UMNO. In the 1980s and towards the end of the 1990s, disunity and factionalism in UMNO became more personified, firstly, as a result of the Mahathir-Tengku Razaleigh[3] contest for party positions, which saw the establish-ment of a splinter group from UMNO called Semangat 46 (later dissolved) and the sacking of Anwar Ibrahim on 2 September 1998, which subsequently created the rift, split and contestations between Tun Dr. Mahathir Mohamad and Dato' Seri Anwar Ibrahim for power and influence in the late 1990s (1998/1999). UMNO began to experience the weakening of group feeling, loyalty and solidarity within the party, in a typical scenario described by Ibn Khaldun in his political theory of regime change. Nevertheless, UMNO still did not read these as indicators of decline of its political influence and power base.

It should be appreciated that the period of the 1990s coincided also with the growing awareness and consciousness of the public on the importance of civil society in many developing countries in shaping and sustaining democracy. It was also, at this time, that we saw the arrival of the digital age and the critical role played by the digital media becoming more emphatic in society and politics. Consistent with this development, it could be seen that demands were made for a more comprehensive political and economic reforms in the country, especially following the dismissal of Anwar Ibrahim as the DPM and Deputy President of UMNO in September 1998 by Tun Mahathir.

---

[3] In this contest, Mahathir won the UMNO President's post by 40 just votes and Ghafar Baba won the position of Deputy President against Musa Hitam by nearly the same number of votes (43). Razaleigh and Rais Yatim formed a new party called 'Semangat 46'. The Court declared UMNO illegal on an action taken by Tengku Razaleigh and his faction.

The voices of dissent were noticeably more explicit and difficult to contain. Anwar's removal had a negative impact on the 1999 election results for UMNO, especially in the Malay heartlands. Tun Mahathir was so disappointed with the Malay voters' support for Anwar during this election. However, BN managed to get two-thirds majority in the Parliament due to the support of the non-Malay voters. In the subsequent delineation of election boundaries, Tun Mahathir decided to adopt the approach of more mixed constituencies to reflect the multi-racial composition of the country. From then on, the non-Malay components of the votes in constituencies increased, more importantly and often becoming the determinant votes in the urban and semi-urban areas even where the Malays were the majority. This allowed for the expression of stronger and louder dissenting voices as per the need for broader space for freedom and democracy in Malaysia. During the leadership of Tun Abdullah Ahmad Badawi as the PM, the voice of the opposition became louder. Tun Abdullah opened up a wider platform for freedom of expression and democracy, which changed the political and social environment.

In the 1959 election, feeling ignored by post-independence economic and educational policies, approximately 50% of Malays voted for the Pan Malayan Islamic Party (PMIP), giving it 13 parliamentary seats and control of two state governments: Kelantan and Terengganu. A decade later, Malay support for PAS was at a similar level, for the same reasons. PAS gained 12 parliamentary seats, won the state assembly convincingly in Kelantan and fell just short in Terengganu (11 of 24 seats). Non-Malay voters helped the opposition secure assembly wins in Penang and Perak, and equal seats in Selangor. Technically, the Alliance failed to win 50 per cent of the popular vote or secure a two-thirds parliamentary majority, but it did gain both three days after voting concluded when a minor Sarawak party agreed to join the Alliance coalition. Before post-election realignments, the Alliance obtained 48.6% of the vote for the peninsula and 47.6% for Malaysia as a whole. But the reality of support for the Alliance was greater, because in the areas where it had strong support it won nine peninsula seats and 20 Malaysia-wide seats that were uncontested (Funston, 2018).

In 1999, the non-Malay electorate handed the BN a comfortable win (148 of 193 seats), but UMNO had its worst result ever. For the first time, the BN faced a united Barisan Alternative (Alternative Front) (BA) that brought together the main opposition parties: the predominantly Chinese DAP, the Malay-Islamist PAS and the new interracial National Justice Party (Parti Keadilan Nasional, Keadilan or PKN) linked to former Deputy Prime Minister (DPM) Anwar Ibrahim. In the wake of Tun Mahathir's sacking and jailing of Anwar, and the arrival of the '*reformasi*' movement, UMNO's parliamentary seats declined from 94 (89 elected in 1995) to 72. PAS achieved its best result ever, winning 27 seats, and as part of the BA retained power in Kelantan and regained Terengganu. Less than half the Malay vote went to UMNO, with some accounts suggesting this was below 40%, according to Datuk Azmi Khalid, Minister for Rural Development (*Berita Harian*, 2000, as cited in Roslan 2001: 20). Kamarudin Jaffar has estimated 70% of Malays voted against UMNO (Roslan 2001).

In 2008, DAP, PAS and Keadilan cooperated in a loose coalition. They won 82 parliamentary seats, leaving the government with 140, short of the important two-thirds majority. Opposition parties also won power in five states (Kelantan, Kedah, Penang, Selangor and Perak—although they soon lost the latter when three assembly persons changed sides). Having achieved its best result ever in the preceding 2004 election, BN slumped to its worst result ever.

In 2013, the same three opposition parties united as the People's Alliance (Pakatan Rakyat, PR) won 89 seats, again leaving BN short of a two-thirds majority. More importantly, PR won the popular vote with 50.9% to the BN's 47.4%. At the state level, it lost Kedah and Terengganu but maintained its hold over Kelantan, Penang and Selangor. Najib blamed the result on a "Chinese tsunami", but in both 2008 and 2013 urban Malays also made a major contribution to opposition gains. Taking the data from the preceding three elections, namely 2008, UMNO had 79 seats (56%) of the total seats of 140 seats won by BN. In 2013, the figure dwindled further downwards, though UMNO gained an extra 9 seats to bring it to 88 (66.19%) of BN; however, its total of 133 seats was less than its seats in the 2008 GE. In 2018, GE14 dropped to 54 (68.35) of BN's total seats of 79 seats. This is in terms of total parliamentary seats equivalent to UMNO's share of total number of seats 21.10% (Moniruzzaman and Farzana 2018: 217).

Malay voters, though they generally voted along ethnic lines, were no longer necessarily monolithic or remained permanently loyal to UMNO as shown in previous election results (Funston 2018). They were quite willing to shift their support to other Malay political parties as an expression of their dissatisfaction with the ruling party. Funston in his analysis of the Malay voting pattern concludes that though on the surface statistics showed overwhelming majority of the Malays supported UMNO, there has been volatility in their support depending on the issues and contexts. In 1959, over economic and educational issues, 50% of Malay votes shifted to PAS, resulting in PAS gaining an extra 13 parliamentary seats and becoming the ruling party in two state governments, namely Terengganu and Kelantan (Funston 2018).

In 1969, during which the 13 May tragedy and racial riots occurred, PAS gained 12 parliamentary seats, won Kelantan with a fantastic majority and lost Terengganu by a very narrow margin (obtained 11 state seats out of 24—PAS needed 13 seats to retain the state of Terengganu). On the other hand, the opposition won the states of Penang and Perak because of non-Malay votes, and in Selangor, the government and opposition obtained equal votes. In this election, the Alliance failed to have 50% of the popular votes or two-thirds majority in Parliament until a minor Sarawak party decided to join the Alliance coalition. In terms of total votes, the Alliance obtained 48.6% of the vote in Peninsular Malaysia and 47.6% for the whole country. Moreover, in reality, in the Alliance stronghold constituencies, its support was greater than what was shown by the statistics, taking into account the number of seats it won uncontested, nine in peninsular and 20 seats nationwide (Funston 2018: 58–59).

In the 1999 elections, the Anwar-Mahathir fallout further ruptured the Malay unity and widening of factionalism.[4] Consequently, UMNO recorded its worst result ever in the Malay majority constituencies. It was obvious that a substantial number of Malay voters' support went to Anwar and his newly formed PKR. Any Malay disunity would be reflected in the election results of the political party, whose leader they supported. The emergence of disunity and factionalism within UMNO affected the support of the Malay voters, and it also weakened loyalty and unity of the party. During the election, UMNO's Malay votes were reduced. The split between Anwar and Tun Mahathir saw the birth of PKR and the reformation movement. In the 1999 GE, Anwar adopted coalition politics similar to the BN and, for the first time, the BN faced a united opposition front called BA comprising DAP (Chinese), PAS (Malay/ Muslim) and Parti Keadilan Nasional (National Justice Party). Anwar led BA against Tun Mahathir's BN in the elections. Anwar was charged with the offence of sodomy, found guilty and jailed. The dismissal of Anwar prompted the formation of a new civil movement called *'Reformasi'*.

Using the united opposition platform, the new opposition coalition partners under Barisan Alternatif (BA) contested the GE against UMNO in 1999 and 2004, which impacted the total number of seats UMNO could garner. It showed a decline of UMNO's seats from 94 in 1990 to 89 seats in the 1995 election. The number of parliamentary seats was further eroded in 1999, when UMNO managed to secure only 72 parliamentary seats. UMNO's erosion of electoral support was an advantage to PAS, who obtained the best result ever by winning 27 parliamentary seats. The swing of Malay votes enabled PAS under the PA to retain Kelantan and regain Terengganu. In terms of the number of votes, UMNO seemed to capture less than 40% (72 seats or 29.7% of the Malay votes (Teik, 2010; Malaysia Parliamentary Chamber: Dewan Rakyat, Election Held in 1999), while MCA contributed 28 seats or 14.06% of the votes, MIC 7 seats or 2.58% of the votes polled, while Sabah and Sarawak contributed 41 seats or 10.40% giving the BN its two-thirds majority or total votes polled of 56.57%. Refer to Figs. 4.3 and 4.4 below on last GE14 Results:

The trend of decline was very visible and the opposition came nearer and nearer to gaining political power, simply due to the split in Malay votes. In the 1999 GE, UMNO in fact would have lost the government to BA if not for the support of the non-Malay electorate. This gave UMNO and BN a comfortable majority of 2/3 with 148 seats out of the total 193 parliamentary seats.

These ups and downs of voters' support in terms of Malay voters towards UMNO were caused by disunity, factionalism, unfair distribution of benefits within the Malay society, cronyism and unfavourable policy initiatives that affected the well-being of the Malay community, and there was a sense of being marginalised in what they called their own country. UMNO did not address these dissatisfactions and was perceived to have failed in upholding Malay positions. The Malay vote swing caused UMNO

---

[4] Anwar as deputy to Mahathir has always trajected his own image locally and internationally. Often he made policy statements that seem to sound and look different from Mahathir. He took over the position of Deputy President and DPM on a sweeping populist votes of the party and of the electorates.

| Party | Pakatan Harapan. Sabah Heritage Party | Barisan Nasional | Gagasan Sejahtera |
|---|---|---|---|
| Last Election. | 68 seats, 37.1% | 133 seats, 47.38% | 21 seats, 14.78% |
| | (Pakatan Rakyat) | | (Pakatan Rakyat) |
| Seats won | 121 | 79 | 18 |
| Seat change | ↑53 | ↓54 | ↓3 |
| Popular vote | 5,781,600 | 4,080,797 | 2,051,188 |
| Percentage | 47.92% | 33.80% | 16.99% |
| Swing | ↑10.82% | ↓13.58% | ↑2.21% |

**Fig. 4.3**  The Result of GE14 (*Source* Moniruzzaman & Farzana [2018])

| | | Vote | | Seats | | |
|---|---|---|---|---|---|---|
| | | Votes | % | Won | % | +/− |
| Barisan Nasional | BN | 4,080,797 | 33.80 | 79 | 35.59 | ↓54 |
| United Malays National Organisation | UMNO | 2,548,251 | 21.10 | 54 | 24.32 | ↓34 |
| United Traditional Bumiputera Party | PBB | 220,479 | 1.83 | 13 | 5.86 | ↓1 |
| Sarawak People's Party | PRS | 59,218 | 0.49 | 3 | 1.35 | ↓3 |
| Malaysian Indian Congress | MIC | 167,061 | 1.39 | 2 | 1.35 | ↓2 |
| Progressive Democratic Party | PDP | 59,853 | 0.50 | 2 | 0.90 | ↓2 |
| 5 parties 1 seat each- MCA SUPP PBS UPKO | PBRS | 925,823 | 7.29 | 5 | 2.25 | ↓11 |
| 3 other parties- Gerakan LDP myPPP | | 145,391 | 1.20 | 0 | 0 | ↓1 |

**Fig. 4.4**  BN Partners' Electoral Performance (*Source* Moniruzzaman & Farzana [2018])

to lose its dominant position and no effective or proactive action was taken to prevent the decline from continuing. From the several Malay vote swings, it can be said that voters' loyalty is not static and has its own dynamics as well as not necessarily fixed to UMNO. Malay votes have shifted several times depending on the outstanding Malay issues that were not resolved by the party or government, generally on leadership. The Malay voters would move to other Malay-based parties and in some cases even to the DAP, especially on issues of governance, corruption and leadership's failure.

These symptoms on voters' sentiment and support were actually discernible and widely discussed within and outside UMNO circles, in public and vigorously in the digital media space, before the elections. The results of the 2008 and 2013 elections would give the best indicators, in instances such as the reduction of percentage of popular votes obtained by UMNO, the number of seats won during the elections, the disappearance of the two-thirds majority in Parliament and also the loss of some of the state governments. Since the 2008 and 2013 GEs, the non-Malay voters had moved away from the UMNO coalition. They would not come back to support UMNO/BN on the grounds that Tun Abdullah and Najib did not deracialise political and policy initiatives as well as their failure to contain corruption.

Najib who succeeded Abdullah in April 2009 strongly believed his different style of leadership and new policy initiatives could reverse the political fortune of UMNO. Due to the weakness of the coalition partners of BN in the peninsular and the abandonment of non-Malay voters of BN[5] due to Najib's over-playing of Malay sentiments and even with the use of coercion, the non-Malay voters' preference did not change. While Najib was able to increase the UMNO seats, he was not able to influence Malaysian voters as a whole as he had image and trust deficits in multiple areas, including politics and economics, governance, corruption, cronyism and campaign missteps.[6] In addition, he faced a more determined, united and confident PR opposition. He won the election of 2013 with a reduced majority. UMNO and its coalition partners won only 133 parliamentary seats out of 222, less than what Tun Abdullah obtained in 2008. Regrettably, Najib did not see the need for him to abdicate his position as President of UMNO and PM of Malaysia even though he did far worse than Tun Abdullah. It should be noted that Najib was not forced out because he had placed his men not only in the Cabinet, but in the Supreme Council of UMNO and at the division levels. UMNO's/BN's refusal to read the writing on the wall and the warning signs of voters' discontent in the party and Najib himself as a leader was a grave and costly mistake for UMNO.

GE12, 2008, according to William Case (2010) is the most studied election in the context of Southeast Asia. Analysis by different scholars, such as Graham Brown (2008); Kee Thuan Chye (2008); Maznah Mohamad (2008); Ong Kian Ming (2008); Ooi Kee Beng *et. al.* (2008); Andreas Ufen (2008); Bridget Welsh (2008); James Chin and Wong Chin Huat (2009); Abdul Rashid Moten (2006); Thomas Pepinsky (2009); and William Case (2010), gave an excellent overview on why voters went against UMNO, and hence, BN suffered a severe slide at the back of its glorious victory in 2004. In sum, it can be said that it was due to Tun Abdullah's failure to deliver his pledges on politics, the economy, governance corruption and cronyism. In the case of Najib, his failure to read the outcome of GE13 and vacate the post of UMNO's President prior to GE14 costs the party and the BN government dearly. These factors caused the voters swing to the detriment of UMNO, its leader and the government.

As a result of the aforesaid setbacks and voter perceptions on Abdullah's performance and leadership, the 2008 election indicated the popular vote of the BN government decreased from approximately 60% of the total, which it normally obtained,

---

[5] At the 2013 GE, the coalition partners of BN had lost almost all support from non-Malays. In fact, Najib got so disappointed with Chinese voters that immediately after the results, he made a statement asking what more do the Chinese want? The researcher went to see Najib and informed him the only way he could recover is to work out a new formula with the DAP. This was rejected on the basis the MCA had been with UMNO since independence and he would not abandon them now.

[6] 1MDB and SRC alleged financial scandals and abuse of power cases by Najib as a PM and Finance Minister.

to a bare majority nationally of 51.2% in the peninsular. The party leadership was shocked to have only 140 parliamentary seats out of the total (of which UMNO's share of the seats fell from 109 to a mere 79 seats) 222 parliamentary seats. For the first time since 1969, BN lost its two-thirds majority. Worst still, the opposition captured five state governments (Perak was subsequently recaptured due to defections). There was also a 5% Malay votes' swing against UMNO. Surprisingly, these votes instead of going to PAS went to PKR and in some constituencies shifted to the DAP (Brown 2008; Ong 2008). Ong Kian Ming's study indicates the patterns of votes obtained by each party in Peninsular Malaysia: BN obtained 58% of Malay votes, 35% of Chinese votes and only 48% of Indian votes particularly due to the influence of the HINDRAF (Hindu Rights Action Force) (Ong 2018). BN usually had very high voter scores among Indians. Some citizens suggested that these shifts might be reflecting a new phenomenon of cross-ethnic unity.

The coalition called Pakatan Rakyat (PR) led by Anwar was seen to have a cross-ethnic appeal, and possibly, the voters might have considered them as a possible viable alternative for change. This was the sign of the appearance of a viable alternative coalition politics in Malaysia, facilitated by Anwar. However, this coalition was not strong enough to upset UMNO. The extra parliamentary seats of BN were contributed by Sabah and Sarawak, referred to by BN leaders as bonus—of 55 seats out of the total 57 parliamentary seats, which gave BN a credible majority to form the government.

Najib and his faction, seeing the weaknesses of Tun Abdullah's government and support, quickly seized the opportunity to make his political move among the senior party leadership, government leaders, media and grassroots. In fact, Tun Abdullah was forced to step aside to enable Najib to succeed. This was said to be necessary for the sake of the party and government. Tun Abdullah was blamed for UMNO's poor performance and was forced to step down as Prime Minister (Gomez and Kaur 2014). The non-confrontational Tun Abdullah against the advice of his close aides acquiesced to Najib's demand and through various intermediaries[7] from both sides negotiated the appropriate time for the handover of the premiership after one year from the election in April 2009. Things proceeded as planned by Najib and the transfer of power proceeded without any hitch.

Najib quickly placed his men in the party and Cabinet to regain public and party confidence. He, as the PM, fully realised that he faced a serious threat from another coalition political group that could take over the federal government by showing they had the capacity to govern at the state level and were, hence, capable of ruling at the federal level. In order to quickly recover and project a trans-ethnic political image, Najib introduced his 1Malaysia slogan as a unification tool for the nation. He addressed the plight of the poor Malay population centres through numerous policies and took necessary measures to overcome the global financial crisis. He had to undertake what was seen as race-based policies in areas where the opposition had secured strong presence, in reality to address the hard-core poverty among the *Bumiputera* states in Sabah, Kelantan, Perlis and Kedah. In this regard, he mentioned that the

---

[7] The researcher was one of the intermediaries between the two sides to ensure a smooth transition of power.

policies were aimed to protect and promote the interests of the *Bumiputera* community for his own UMNO constituents, when in fact these were national problems that needed to be resolved.

Najib wanted, upon taking over the helm of party and government, to distinguish himself from Tun Abdullah's regime. He pledged, *inter alia*, to end rent seeking and patronage, and to minimise regional and social inequities. While these new policies were credible and good for overcoming the economic, political and social problems and challenges faced by the *rakyat* and country, he had to deal with new problems. News began to appear and circulate involving corporate scandals of government-controlled companies with well-connected business people linked to BN politicians that had brought lucrative profits. In spite of his pledge to curb patronage, major projects were privatised selectively. The problems of money politics in UMNO continued to inundate the party and financial scandals and corruption had not been abated. For example, there was the continuous speculation and often public knowledge of abuse of power by Taib Mahmud, the Chief Minister of Sarawak, amassing enormous wealth. Najib himself was alleged to be involved in receiving enormous kickbacks in acquisition of defence equipment and on many other similar acts, prior to GE13. This was, of course, contrary to what he pledged to do immediately after taking over the leadership from Tun Abdullah.

In spite of what he said on stopping rent seeking and patronage, he had four years to implement his reform programmes, prior to GE13 in May. No doubt Najib presented an impressive BN 2013 manifesto; nonetheless, the electorate remained unconvinced with Najib's transformation agenda. As a result of lack of voters' support, he did worse than the GE12 under Tun Abdullah. He secured only 133 parliamentary seats, compared to Tun Abdullah's 140 seats in GE12, and popular votes were less than 50%. However, Najib hired the best image and PR consultant who did a clever spin by saying he did well because he gained back nine seats for UMNO that increased its representation from 79 seats in the Parliament to 88 (refer to Tables above). Hitherto, he did not face internal revolt as he had also made sure the UMNO parliamentarians were his men or the common knowledge circulating that the candidates were those endorsed by his wife (these comments and remarks about the wife of the PM are common knowledge among party members, professionals and people from all walks of life in the country).

UMNO as a single party still had the largest number of seats in the Dewan Rakyat (Lower House of parliament). The GE13 was a repeat of the voting pattern of GE12. In urban areas, BN suffered its biggest defeats among the middle-class electorate and had a slight edge from the number of seats obtained by PR in the Malay majority areas. In order to have a credible majority, again Sabah and Sarawak enabled the BN to retain the federal government in Putrajaya. In terms of popular votes (though under the electoral first past the post system this does not count much), there were good indicators of the level of electoral support for the BN that it should have taken notice of. In GE13, nationally, BN lost the popular votes, by obtaining only 49% nationwide and in the peninsular 43%. Additionally, PR retained Selangor and Penang and made huge inroads into Johore, while retaining Kelantan.

In addition, the government was also troubled by high inflation and unemployment. Across the three communities, 31% of Malays, 20% of Chinese and 26% of Indians were unhappy at the rising costs of living (Merdeka Centre, 2018 as cited in Hutchinson and Lee 2019). UMNO leaders at all levels of the grassroots felt the heat and anger of their traditional electoral supporters. UMNO constituents were weakening, while their party leaders were unable to inspire them. UMNO began to experience problems when its leaders relied on racial branding in order to gain legitimacy from the Malay masses. The party started to infuse fear of the others, such as without UMNO there is no future for the Malays and if it is not in power, the so-called concept of "*Ketuanan Melayu*" (Malay dominance) would fade forever (for a further detailed account of this subject, see Welsh [2018b]). The intention was to raise emotions and support. This type of battle cry was something Tun Mahathir had disallowed to encourage the non-Malay entrepreneurship into his industrialisation policy. With Tun Abdullah's policy of greater space for freedom and free speech, surprisingly, this divisive call was allowed to continue unabated. For example, the over-Malayness expression was further demonstrated during the UMNO Youth Assemblies in 2006 and 2007. Hishamuddin Tun Hussein Onn, who led the UMNO Youth as well as the Ministry of Education, drew out a *keris* (Malay dagger) as an indication of the need for Malay ascendancy (Jaymal 2008). During GE13 and GE14, the rhetoric of UMNO was "*Ketuanan Melayu*" (Malay dominance) and did not go down well with the non-Malay voters. In instilling fear about the threat of others, Hishamuddin garnered the support and created excitement and emotions among the UMNO youth delegates. The speeches that followed the incident at the assembly reaffirmed their commitment to the "Malay Agenda" (Lee and Nesadurai 2010). This was widely published in the print and electronic media. The action of the Youth Leader was truly populist and counter-productive. It alienated further the non-Malay electorate, whose support at this time was already low. This was one of the main causes of UMNO and BN electoral setback in GE12 (Pepinsky 2009).[8]

With economic development and government policies, a middle class was created in the urban and rural areas. This had brought about a shift of political culture and attitudes among the voters. UMNO failed to recognise this shift. According to Edmund Terence Gomez and Surinder Kaur (2014: 1), "UMNO's influence in society has been steadily eroding since 2008, seen in its overwhelming rejection by the urban middle class and some segment of rural Malays". Because of the growing maturity of the Malaysian democracy, they had more space for freedom and open discussions; hence, they were more ready to vote according to what they thought was right. The voters were more conscious and aware of their rights and what was happening around them. It could be said that since 2008, the public became more critical on issues of transparency, governance and accountability, and on issues of corruption, lifestyle and character of candidates.

---

[8] The Keris episode by Hishamuddin, a Minister in the Cabinet and UMNO Youth Leader, further damaged UMNO and its coalition partner in BN among non-Malay voters, especially the Chinese. Abdullah as the PM and leader of BN did not reprimand Hishamuddin, opting instead to defend him. Both Malay and non-Malay voters were disappointed with his leadership. They showed their anger in the 2008 election (Case 2010).

Furthermore, warlords at the division levels prevented new young and educated UMNO members from succeeding in the UMNO hierarchy. There was a tendency at the branch and division levels for them to keep on holding on to positions in order to continue receiving material and financial benefits. It would not be unusual for tainted and corrupt candidates to continue being re-nominated for state or parliamentary seats in spite of the leaders' loud political rhetoric to control patronage and corruption. The voice and feedback of the grassroots in 2013 were not listened to and the party fielded candidates with blemished character and reputation, so long as they were the leader's man/woman (these are the voices of members' dissatisfaction silently expressed at all levels of the party membership… from the researcher's personal knowledge speaking to members). This often made it impossible or at times difficult to get the electorate to vote for BN. In retrospect, Tun Mahathir had a way of controlling the warlords, but subsequent prime ministers were perceived to allow it to exist at the state and federal levels to ensure their own survival. UMNO presidents were very much under the influence of the powerful factional leaders. UMNO members were dissatisfied with Tun Abdullah and Najib for not practising fair and just distribution of benefits, which instead were distributed to their cronies (individuals and companies associated with party leaders) (Case 2010).

Additionally, Dato' Sri Najib bin Tun Abdul Razak as the leader of UMNO at this time was seen to be ineffective due to his unwillingness to listen to the sentiments of members, perceived to be corrupt and living in opulence and luxury as well as aloof and complacent about the ills of the party (Brown 2018; Gunasegaram and Kinibiz 2018; Wright and Hope 2018). Bridget Welsh (2018a: 86) says, "Najib's involvement in the world's largest kleptocracy scandal to date, 1Malaysia Development Berhad (1MDB), was an integral part of voter alienation, especially in urban areas". Political loyalty was blemished among Malays and this brought about an important change in ethnic support which also plunged UMNO into crisis as the party whose leader abused the power, and became embroiled in money politics of billions of Ringgit. "GE14 should thus be seen as a UMNO tsunami, as change in voting patterns point to a decimation of the party's political base" (Welsh 2018b: 98). Funston (2018) blames Najib for the loss of support to the incumbent party in GE14 due to the corruption scandals and unwillingness to address political reform. Finally, the researcher would like to quote an article written by Liew Chin Tong (2019) in *New Straits Times* in which he said, "… I have always reminded friends and supporters of Pakatan Harapan that we must humbly accept the fact we did not win the 2018 election on our strength alone. It was former prime minister Datuk Seri Najib Razak and his wife, Datin Seri Rosmah Mansor, who lost it for Barisan Nasional (BN)".

When analysing the symptoms of declining support for UMNO, the results of GE12, GE13 and GE14 were used as benchmarks to understand the behaviour of the voters. Factors and symptoms indicated the decline such as the loss of two-thirds majority and the big reductions of popular votes. Therefore, UMNO could no longer claim it was the dominant political party in Malaysian politics. Hence, it is quite true to emphasise that their political position was under threat. In order to overcome this decline and loss of dominion, UMNO had to make a fundamental structural transformation. The question is whether they could or were willing to do so to prevent further decline after the GE13. After the negative performance in 2008, no fundamental change was made, other than removing Tun Abdullah as President and Prime Minister, which was quite well planned and executed by Najib. Similarly, after performing worse than Tun Abdullah in 2013, Najib continued as President of UMNO and Prime Minister of Malaysia. He knew UMNO needed reform of the party and policy; however, he proceeded with business as usual and no metamorphosis of any kind was undertaken in UMNO. From GEs in 2008 and 2013, the electorates' message and narrative was for change in the political order and system.

Nonetheless, as said by Ibn Khaldun, the ruler living in comfort and economic success did not listen to the voices of the ruled. The public wanted rule of law, governance, end to patronage and rent seeking, cronyism, warlordism as well as better space for freedom and democracy. The people wanted to transform society and politics in order to shape a new Malaysian nation based on rule of law and justice. Under these circumstances, the only way forward was regime change through the ballot box. The opposition PH presented themselves as a capable alternative to the UMNO-led government in the GEs of 2008 and 2013. The opposition made credible inroads at the parliamentary and state levels, but they were not strong or cohesive enough to overturn the government until GE14 with a new coalition politics headed by the former Prime Minister Tun Mahathir.

## 4.3   The Factors Behind Decline of UMNO: The Erosion of the Malay *'asabiyyah*

The previous section discusses symptoms of UMNO's decline from power and dominance. There was sufficient existential evidence to show that UMNO's influence and voters' support were declining and this trend was demonstrated, especially in the outcomes of the 2008 and 2013 elections. Talking about this decline, Tun Mahathir says: "Call me a racist but Malays are in decline and it's our fault" (Malaysiakini 2018). Therefore, UMNO's factors of decline can be inferred from the visible symptoms of its decline. Given Ibn Khaldun's view that decline of civilisations followed a social and historical pattern, this means that the absence of the factors that were socially and historically responsible for the rise of a civilisation if absent becomes the cause of its decline. Therefore, Ibn Khaldun concluded that the cohesive existence of *'asabiyyah* and its corollary concept of political leadership that plays a role in its formation are the cause for rise of a civilisation, and its erosion will result in the decline and erosion of that given civilisation. Hence, the Malay *'asabiyyah* and political leadership were socially and historically the cause of the rise and dominance of UMNO in the politics of Malaysia, and the erosion of the Malay *'asabiyyah* and corruption of leadership in UMNO are the historical causes of the decline of UMNO. This can be explained as follows.

No doubt, UMNO is the oldest political party with vast knowledge, experience and records of successes in the political and economic history of Malaysia. At the beginning of its rise and growth, the Malays were held together and united under the banner of UMNO by what can be considered as *'asabiyyah.* Technically, there was this group feeling, cohesion and solidarity to achieve a common objective and interest in defeating the British MU Constitution and achieving independence. It was the group feeling, solidarity, unity and cohesion that enabled the Malays to have the sense of cultural togetherness as Malayan instead of *'semangat kenegerian'.* Leaders of the Malays in UMNO motivated them to work together to seek independence for Malaysia.

As a result of this struggle, they obtained *mulk* (power) and authority under a coalition formula by way of negotiation and diplomacy with the British and with the ethnic Chinese and Indian by coalition politics of power sharing. The British and state rulers recognised that they had popular support and strength. Additionally, the government with the support of the people and the help of the British was able to fight against the armed communist insurgencies because of the people's trust and confidence in bringing peace and justice. The UMNO-led alliance administered the country and government, which brought economic development and progress to all Malaysians. The leaders and party practised good governance, rule of law and justice and managed the nation with sincerity and honesty that attained peace and political stability.

Since independence, they were given the mandate to govern in thirteen successive elections. The leadership of BN considered they had brought change and benefits to the people, exercised fairness and justice, and initiated policies for the good of the people and nation; thus, the electorate should support them to power. In Ibn Khaldun's analysis, *'asabiyyah* is the concept of the presence of strong group feeling based on unity, loyalty, social cohesion and strong solidarity. *'asabiyyah* would succeed not because of blood relations only but the ability of the group to identify a common interest with fellow members of the social organisation. Under UMNO, the Malays nationwide became a tightly knit group that showed solidarity, loyalty to each other and most importantly their preparedness to sacrifice their individual to group interest. It was this same group feeling that enabled them to defend, protect and promote their claims and rights in the country.

Due to the successes and economic growth and development, UMNO took things for granted and neglected its responsibility to the country and *rakyat.* The leaders at all levels of BN became complacent, living in luxury and opulent urban centres and took things for granted on dispensing justice, while morality and ethical conduct edged closer to decadence. Once the social cohesion begins to drift and dwindle, unity, decay and individual greed, avarice and corruption become an integral part of government. In this context, the public associated UMNO with a party of greed, cronyism, corruption and individual interest, incompetent leaders with glaring examples of misdeeds and unwillingness to change.

Due to these reasons, UMNO became completely out of touch with the realities on the ground affecting the people. It acquired the elitist character and behaviour with very feudalistic traits of self-aggrandisement.[9] There was a strong feeling of discomfort that UMNO leaders were dominating the *rakyat*. In order to sustain their positions, they continued to encourage the rent-seeking activities, patronage, cronyism, warlordism with a touch of egoism and self-interest. Rightly, Ibn Khaldun suggested regime change occurs as processes that undermine the political entities, whereby strong and charismatic leadership is overturned into an effete, rent-seeking administration and, thus, lose the loyalty of the electorate. This, in itself, made UMNO vulnerable to the encroachment of a new coalition that is perceived as just and fair in meeting the needs of the people.

In Ibn Khaldun's political theory of leadership, many leaders fail due to inability or because they ignore the significance of *'asabiyyah*. Ibn Khaldun (1974) indicated cooperation in order to work depends on a restraining influence, which is the phenomenon of leadership. "To him "leadership … is inevitable" and people in varying degrees have a readiness to accept leadership. Leadership cannot emerge without the adoption of *'asabiyyah* or group feeling" (Sidani 2008: 77). Hence, UMNO's rise and fall, the role of Malay *'asabiyyah* and UMNO's leaders in formation of Malay's *'asabiyyah* fit well into Ibn Khaldun's theory of *'asabiyyah* and the five stages of rise and fall of *'umran*. In Ibn Khandun's view, *'asabiyyah* interacts with *'umran* through five stages and moves society and life towards the *'umranic* lifestyle or causes the decline of the *'umranic* life. They are: (1) conquest: this is based on strong feelings of *'asabiyyah* that produces an irresistible strength among the tribesmen; (2) single ruler: emergence of a charismatic, respected leader; (3) broadly popular rule—the period when the leaders draw strength from the group; (4) over-confidence: the ruler becomes complacent and cut off from the majority of population. The ruler becomes reclusive and surrounds himself with most loyal servants. Population has become sedentary and accustomed to the luxuries of city life; and (5) collapse: new underdog tribal group seizes control. Their togetherness gives them the edge.

Therefore, the Malay *'asabiyyah* exists in every stage of UMNO's development, but the degree of its effectiveness varied from high to low and it very much depended on the UMNO leadership. The stronger and just the UMNO leader, the stronger and more durable was its hold on power. When the Malay *'asabiyyah* was high or strong, UMNO was able to pull Malaysia towards the *'umranic* stage of development, but UMNO began to decline when the Malay *'asabiyyah* began to erode, thanks to the complacency of the political leadership of UMNO, Najib and his team of ministers, who lost the sense of humility, sincerity and honesty that early leaders of UMNO possessed and practised.

On 9 May 2018, the UMNO-led government lost the election to the PH coalition. Serina Rahman (2018) describes the defeat of UMNO-led government as a Tsunami Rakyat and the dawn of a new era. She, however, argues that the description of a Malay Tsunami should not be overemphasised. The outcome was not a dislike

---

[9] In a number of instances, the researcher spoke with a few members of the Cabinet, who are also members of the UMNO Supreme Council to highlight the many indicators of dissatisfaction among voters and at the grassroots. However, all such warnings were ignored.

for UMNO but more as a protest vote against Najib Razak, his family and party leaders over their arrogance and conspicuous overspending habits. Added to this is the unpopular introduction of the goods and sales tax (GST), which caused inflation and hardships for the ordinary men and women on the street.

True to what Ibn Khaldun (1974: 101) said "… leadership exists only through superiority, and superiority only through group feeling. Leadership over people, therefore, must, of necessity, derive from a group feeling that is superior to each individual group feeling. Each individual group feeling that becomes aware of their superiority of the group feeling of the leader is ready to obey and follow him" (as cited in Yusuf Sidani 2008: 78–79). What Ibn Khaldun said in the fourteenth century and in a different era is relevant to what happened to UMNO.

## 4.4  Conclusion

This chapter discusses the symptoms and factors that led to the decline and loss of power of UMNO. It incorporates explanation of the symptoms and factors or the phenomena that led to the decline of UMNO. Symptoms of the decline of UMNO were evident as early as in 2008 during GE12. These election results consistently suggested the decline in voter support. The UMNO leaders did not pay attention to the situation and did not introduce political and structural reforms. They remained overconfident and employed the method of fear to remind the Malays that their fate was closely connected with UMNO's political fate. The Malays had become disenchanted and Malays' support of UMNO gradually eroded. If anything, that could explain the collapse of UMNO's power; much is attributed to the leadership of Najib, as President and his UMNO colleagues in the party and the Cabinet. UMNO, if it wants to regain the Malays' trust and support, must address the problems of factionalism, blind loyalty, warlordism, cronyism, corruption and absence of shared values.

## References


Brown G (2008) Federal and state elections in Malaysia, March 2008. Elect Stud 27(4):740–744

Brown, Rewcastle Clare (2018) The sarawak report: the inside story of the 1MDB exposé. Lost World Press. Petaling Jaya: Gerakbudaya Enterprise

Case W (2010) Malaysia's 2008 general election—Transition from single-party dominance? J Curr Southeast Asian Aff 29(2):121–156

Chin J, Huat WC (2009) Malaysia's electoral upheaval. J Democr 20(3):71–85

Funston J (2018) Malaysia's 14th General Election (GE14)—The Contest for the Malay Electorate. J Curr Southeast Asian Aff 37(3):57–83. https://doi.org/10.1177/186810341803700304

Gomez ET, Kaur S (2014) Struggling for power: Policies, coalition politics and elections in Malaysia. University of Malaya, Kuala Lumpur

Gunasegaram P, Kinibiz (2018) 1MDB: The scandal that brought down a government. Strategic Information and Research Development Centre, Malaysia

Hutchinson FE, Lee HA (eds) (2019) The defeat of barisan nasional: missed signs or late surge? ISEAS Publishing, Singapore

Ibn Khaldun (1974) in Dawood NJ (Ed.), The Muqaddimah (The Introduction), Princeton University Press, Princeton, NJ, (translated by Franz Rosenthal)

Jaymal, SZ (2008) UMNO's Keris is here to stay. Malaysiakini, 6 November. Available online at: http://www.malaysiakini.com/news/74414

Kassim, Shahidan (2006) UMNO: Satu Kajian Kelangsungan Parti Politik Melayu. PhD. Thesis. Universiti Utara Malaysia. http://etd.uum.edu.my/3655/

Kee Thuan Chye (Ed) (2008) March 8: The day Malaysia woke Up. Subang, Malaysia: Marshall Cavendish

Kessler, Clive (2018) Malaysia's electoral fantasy belies worrying reality. 29 April. East Asia Forum. https://www.eastasiaforum.org/2018/04/29/malaysias-electoral-fantasy-belies-worrying-reality/

Lee HG, & Nesadurai, HES (2010) Political transition in Malaysia: the future of Malaysia's hybrid political regime. In: Mely Caballero-Anthony (ed) Political change, democratic transition and security in Southeast Asia, London and New York: Routledge, pp 97–123

*Malaysiakini* (2018) Call me racist but Malays are in decline and it's our fault—Dr M. 29 December. https://www.malaysiakini.com/news/458169

Mohamad M (2008) Malaysia: Democracy and the end of ethnic politics? Aust J Int Aff 62(4):441–459

Moniruzzaman M, Farzana KF (2018) Malaysia' 14th general election: end of an epoch, and beginning of a new? Intellect Discourse 26(1):207–228

Moten AR (2006) The 2004 general elections in Malaysia: A Mandate to Rule. Asian Surv 46(2):319–340

Ong Kian Ming (2008) "Making sense of the political tsunami". Malaysiakini. 11 March. http://www.malaysiakini.com/news/79604.com

Ong Kian Ming (2018) GE14—A truly Malaysian tsunami. Available online at: https://dapmalaysia.org/statements/2018/05/17/27122/

Ooi Kee Beng, Johan Saravanamuttu, and Lee Hock Guan (2008) March 8: Eclipsing May 13. Singapore: Institute of Southeast Asian Studies.

Pepinsky TB (2009) The 2008 Malaysian elections: an end to ethnic politics? J East Asian Stud 9(1):87–120

Rahman, Serina (2018). "When Malaysian youth take a stand... a wave of change follows". 14 May, ISEAS-Yusuf Ishak's. https://www.iseas.edu.sg/media/commentaries/when-malaysian-youth-take-a-stand-a-wave-of-change-follows-by-serina-rahman/

Roslan AH (2001) Income inequality, poverty and development policy in Malaysia. Universiti Utara Malaysia, Kedah: School of Economics. https://www.semanticscholar.org/paper/Income-Inequality-%2C-Poverty-and-Development-Policy-Roslan/b93d23e72af6e595f549648315f7234ea3bba61c

Sidani Y (2008) Ibn Khaldun of North Africa: An AD 1377 theory of leadership. J Manag Hist 14(1):73–86

Teik KB (2010) Commentary the Malaysian general election of 29 November 1999. Aust J Polit Sci 35(2):305–311. https://doi.org/10.1080/713649324

Tong, Liew Chin (2019) "Premature to do GE15 storyboard". New Straits Times. 29 July. https://www.nst.com.my/opinion/columnists/2019/07/508106/premature-do-ge15-storyboard (accessed on 4 August 2022)

*Today* (2018) Once dominant, Malaysia's BN records lowest-ever vote share of 36.4% in 2018 GE. 11 May. https://www.todayonline.com/malaysian-ge/3642-cent-bn-records-lowest-popular-vote-history (accessed on 3 August 2019)

Ufen A (2008) The 2008 elections in Malaysia: Uncertainties of electoral authoritarianism. Taiwan J Democr 4(1):155–169

Welsh B (2018a) "Saviour" Politics and Malaysia's 2018 electoral democratic breakthrough: rethinking explanatory narratives and implications. J Curr Southeast Asian Aff. 37(3):85–108. https://doi.org/10.1177/186810341803700305

Welsh B (ed) (2018b) The end of UMNO?: essays on Malaysia's dominant party. Strategic Information and Research Development Centre (SIRD), Malaysia

Wright T, Hope B (2018) Billion dollar whale: the man who fooled wall street, hollywood, and the world. Hachette Books, New York

# Chapter 5
# Concluding Remarks and Recommendations

**Abstract** This chapter discusses the findings of the study and offers suggestions for UMNO to rise again and regain its power. On the relevance and applicability of Ibn Khaldun's theory of *'asabiyyah* and *'umran*, one may argue that this theory was crafted in the fourteenth-century environment and may not reflect the exact situation today. However, these principles are still legitimate and can be adjusted to meet the contemporary context, such as cooperation and alliances on the basis of common interests. It is natural for human beings to have social organisation and live together in a society or community under a state structure. *'asabiyyah* can then be applied to produce group feeling and solidarity to bring about positive and beneficial outcomes for the community without abandoning the principles of justice and moderation as propagated in the teachings of Islam.

**Keywords** Leadership · UMNO · The *rakyat*

To conclude, this study, using Ibn Khaldun's theory of *'asabiyyah* and *'umran*, examines the causes of the decline of UMNO due to the erosion of the Malay *'asabiyyah*. The previous chapters, despite their limitations, the research questions and theoretical and methodological orientation of the research, indicate that this study uses Ibn Khaldun's theory of *'asabiyyah* and *'umran* to explain the decline of UMNO's power. Ibn Khaldun's early life, intellectual and socio-political environment and his theory of *'asabiyyah* and *'umran* are discussed. In Ibn Khaldun's view, *'umran* is a human product, but it can come into existence only after human beings formed *'asabiyyah*. And *'asabiyyah* can form when human beings unite to promote justice and well-being of the community. According to Ibn Khaldun, human beings can form *'asabiyyah* and develop a very advanced *'umran* under the guidance of sincere, wise and charismatic leaders. Hence, the leadership plays a very significant role in developing and shaping social institutions and human lifestyle.

The history of UMNO, its establishment and rise to dominance and achievements highlight that UMNO's leaders played a significant role in the rise of UMNO to prominence. UMNO was formed in 1946 and brought different Malay local and parochial social and political organisations and movement into a broader national



S. H. bin Syed Jaafar Albar, *Ibn Khaldun's Theory and the Party-Political Edifice of the United Malays National Organisation*, SpringerBriefs in Political Science, https://doi.org/10.1007/978-981-19-7388-8_5

political party. Its aim was to protect the Malay's rights and freedoms. In fact, it united the Malays and became a major resistance institution against the grand design of Britain's colonial administration in Malaya. UMNO aborted the Britain's MU plan for Malaya and managed to convince the colonial administration to agree to the Federation of Malay States Agreement. UMNO led the nation towards independence in 1957 and developed a policy of accommodation to prepare for the creation of a multi-ethnic, multi-religious and multi-racial federal state. It accepted the Chinese and Indian migrants while it struggled for the rights of Malays. UMNO united the Malays and the Malays sincerely supported it. Personalities and leaders like Dato' Onn Jaafar and Tun Abdul Razak were leading UMNO and were the real champions of the Malays rights and freedoms.

Furthermore, the factors and the symptoms of the decline of UMNO are discussed. The study analyses Malaysia's GEs of 2008 and 2013 to show the erosion of people's support for UMNO. It explains that UMNO was affected by the diseases of arrogance, complacency, factionalism, corruption, etc. These problems eventually led to the erosion of Malays' trust in UMNO. The Malay *'asabiyyah* towards UMNO had faded. Malays felt disenchanted with UMNO. Again, the leadership played an important role. This time, the role of UMNO's leaders was negative and was that of neglect. Engrossed in high-level corruption and crony politics, UMNO's leaders could care less about the rising cost of living and the level of morality. The Malays and Malaysians felt disappointed with UMNO's leadership. Finally, they withdrew their support. The Malay electorate had issues with corrupt UMNO leaders beleaguered with financial scandals, and their tendency to disregard the rule of law. These issues were translated into a firm rejection and this rejection manifested itself in the outcome of GE14, bringing down UMNO's 61-year rule. In reality, this simply demonstrates a victory of a stronger *'asabiyyah* over another. On 9 May 2018, UMNO conceded defeat and handed over power to the PH coalition.

I shall conclude the key findings of the discussions above in this study.

1. On the relevance and applicability of Ibn Khaldun's theory of *'asabiyyah* and *'umran*, one may argue that this theory was crafted in the fourteenth-century environment and may not reflect the exact situation today. However, these principles are still legitimate and can be adjusted to meet the contemporary context, such as cooperation and alliances on the basis of common interests or clientship. It is natural for human beings to have social organisation and live together in a society or community under a state structure. *'Asabiyyah* can then be applied to produce group feeling and solidarity to bring about positive and beneficial outcomes for the community without abandoning the principles of justice and moderation as propagated in the teachings of Islam.

2. The initial discussion in Chapter 2 indicates that Ibn Khaldun's theory of *'asabiyyah* and *'umran* have relevance in contemporary times to what happened to UMNO. UMNO had created group feeling and solidarity of the Malays, allowing it to make UMNO a political platform of their struggles against Britain. The study concludes that UMNO had reached the stage of senility as outlined in Ibn Khaldun's five stages of collapse of state or dynasty. The disappearance of

the sense of *'asabiyyah* as seen in UMNO in the popular perception of the leaders of UMNO and the government since GE11 and GE12 shifted from respect to that of contempt, disgust and to some extent even hatred. It could also be seen that the *rakyat*'s shift coincided with the increasing instances of breaches of the rule of law, injustice and abuse of power at the hands of the government agencies and machineries. This condition is further compounded by the growing political and government weaknesses of those responsible in managing the government. Recurring incidences of what was interpreted by the *rakyat* as injustices brought about the downfall of the incumbent government and UMNO as the dominant political party in Malaysia.

3. UMNO's policies of development and economic growth had brought about urbanisation and shaped the social and cultural heritage of the Malays. It had produced rich as well as poor urban Malays in addition to poor rural Malays. The political attitudes of the Malays within and outside UMNO had changed and become more critical and demanding. Politics had become unpleasant, at times disturbing and problematic for the government to handle. Asyiqin Halim (2012: 275) argues that "the Malays have become more critical, analytic and judgemental in their thinking of political affairs". The rural Malays generally are still loyal to UMNO. The Malay electorate definitely is not monolithic but represents several diverse groups, and some changes have occurred in the political environment of Malaysia and the Malay attitudes.

4. In UMNO and Malaysian politics, the leadership plays a fundamental role in the success of the political party. GE14 created history. Najib's father, Tun Abdul Razak, was one of the founding members of UMNO and the founder of the UMNO-led BN coalition. Ironically, Tun Razak's son, Najib, is considered the cause of the decline and defeat of UMNO. UMNO/BN lost the federal government and 11 of the 13 state governments in GE14.

5. One may ask how a dominant political party as UMNO fell from grace. After 61 years in power and government, the party and its leadership were certain they could not be shaken. True to Ibn Khaldun's theory, UMNO and its leaders were comfortable in their position of power. But the erosion of power was steadily taking place, mainly due to the weak leadership and internal dissent, disunity, factionalism, cronyism, warlordism and over-centralisation of the party. The leadership did not notice or simply ignored the electorate's ability to bring them down. Sultan Nazrin Shah of Perak, a keen observer and honest critic of politics, had sent the right signal and warning when he said at the Conference of Malaysian Judges on 9 April 2008: "… governments can no longer just offer their citizens material wealth. The intangible benefits of development, including an absence of corruption, abuse, and repression, and the protection and enlargement of individual rights and freedoms, are now equally important goods that citizens demand and which governments must deliver" (Sultan Nazrin Shah 2008). Regrettably, Malaysian politics was tainted with issues of corruption and financial scandals, which resulted in social problems, factions and the escalation of polarisation in society.

6. The UMNO ruling elite grew accustomed to power and wealth, became aloof from the mass of society and no longer shared a common purpose. Such attitudes caused the erosion of *'asabiyyah*. Thus, in doing so, the leadership of UMNO with the passing of time became removed from the founding spirit of UMNO, the government and the party grew weaker, and disinterested in good governance, and got further alienated from the feelings and sentiments of the *rakyat*. Hence, the early group feelings, unity and solidarity, strength and objective or *'asabiyyah* in UMNO steadily eroded and disintegrated. When leaders of UMNO at the national, state and grassroots levels forgot their responsibility by acquiring wealth and practicing cronyism, conditions became unbearable for the *rakyat* to accept. The Malay leaders were perceived to have ignored and become insensitive to the interests of the *rakyat*; they became complacent and the leaders became aloof. The researcher remembers that his objection of leaders' appointment of a person who was found guilty of money politics was ignored because the person was closely associated with the leaders and his sets of warlords.

The position of power and dominance of UMNO as a leading political grouping is shown to be in a state of decline. It is time for the Malay community to reflect on what they need to do to be strong and have the ability to participate effectively in the Malaysian political arena. The answer lies in possessing the sense of *'asabiyyah* or group feeling and solidarity to deliberate together, fight and overcome their communal problems. The differences or diversity of background or politics, division and disunity will bring greater problems to the Malay community and Islam. The only way forward, based on this study, is to examine the sense of *'asabiyyah* with positivity to move forward to participate honourably and respectfully in a diverse Malaysia, where competition is tough and intense.

Ibn Khaldun emphasised the personal qualities of the leader which he calls "perfecting details", i.e., "generosity, forgiveness of error, patience and perseverance, hospitality towards guests, maintenance of indigent, patience in unpleasant situations, executions of commitments, respect for the religious law, reverence for old men and teachers, fairness, meekness, consideration to the needs of followers, adherence to the obligations of religious laws, and avoidance of deception and fraud" (Sidani 2008: 79–80). The detailing on leadership as Ibn Khaldun has spelt out in the *Muqaddimah* is of paramount significance to all political parties that aspire to rise and sustain the *mulk* in administering the country for the benefits of the *rakyat*. If UMNO would like to reform itself, these details should be given particular attention.

This study points out that the fading of the sense of *'asabiyyah* will be bad and negative for UMNO specifically and the Malay community generally. Being divided into many differing political parties is not wrong. However, the Malays must identify the issues they have differences on and the issues for which they should stand united. It is important, for example, on issues of religion, education and the economy that the Malays should have a common position. In the event when this cannot be achieved, it would make the Malay community weaker in its competition with the other communities and can result in further political divisions, economic inactivity, social dissatisfaction and religious confusion, and in greater weakness.

In order to be relevant to the current political landscape, there must be a new and serious approach and initiatives for UMNO to take steps to change. UMNO has to examine the primary principles of unity and solidarity and the quality of governance that it should practice. The following recommendations can help UMNO regain the confidence of the *rakyat*, sustain the *'umrani* stage of development that Malaysia has already achieved and obtain the *mulk* (political power).

1. UMNO needs to strengthen the sense of *'asabiyyah* among the leadership, grassroots of UMNO and the Malay electorate based on rule of law and good governance in the context of the multi-ethnic citizens of the country.
2. The leaders of UMNO who are tainted and corrupt must vacate their positions voluntarily; otherwise, they must be removed. This exercise must be treated as a process of renewal, which should be done in a transparent manner. The perceptions on the ground of the party not taking any action against corrupt leaders are negative, damaging and unacceptable from the legal perspective as well as political standpoint. In fact, if nothing is done and the attitude is one of "business as usual", it will cause the party to bleed further. Consequently, UMNO will be rejected by the *rakyat* and significant segments of the urban, middle-class and young members of Malay society. UMNO needs a positive perception and acceptance from the *rakyat* to regain their confidence and trust. In this regard, the leadership of the party should be replaced by young and qualified leaders with integrity, good and high moral values and ethics.
3. The new leaders must possess the positive and constructive spirit as well as humility of the UMNO leaders of the 1940s, 1950s, 1960s up to 1970s—one of sincerity, sacrifice and with full dedication. The courage and selflessness to right the wrongs of the past will put them back on the original struggle of UMNO—one which works for the *rakyat*, like the Malay saying, *"sesat jalan, balik ke pangkal jalan"* (if one has taken the wrong path, then retrace it back to the right path).
4. UMNO must discard the practices of money politics, patronage, rent seeking and warlordism and choose its leaders based on merit, those with sincerity and with strong integrity.
5. UMNO should select leaders with values that reflect the current values of society and who can lead the nation.
6. The current centralisation of power whether at state or federal levels must be abolished with a better structure to ensure that they can act to check and balance any malpractices or missteps of leaders at various levels and connect with the grassroots to have the final say on their leaders.
7. The party must be decentralised and made democratic with a new organisation structure.
8. Finally, UMNO should consider the establishment of an institution for party cadre to be trained and inculcated with good values, morals and ethics. Stern actions can be meted against non-compliance before the party falls into the pit.

# References


Halim AA (2012) The application of Ibn Khaldūn's theory of Asabiyyah to the modern period with special reference to the Malay Muslim community in Malaysia. PhD Thesis. University of Birmingham

Sidani Y (2008) Ibn Khaldun of North Africa: an AD 1377 theory of leadership. J Manag Hist 14(1):73–86

Sultan Nazrin Shah (2008) Regent of Perak Raja Nazrin Shah's address at the Conference of Malaysian Judges. 9 April. The Malaysian Bar. https://www.malaysianbar.org.my/article/news/speeches/speeches/regent-of-perak-raja-nazrin-shah-s-address-at-the-conference-of-malaysian-judges. Accessed on 3 August 2022

# About the Editor

Mansoureh Ebrahimi (Suri), Ph.D., is an Associate Professor and research scholar in modern West Asian Studies, Persian literature, language, Eastern and Islamic History and Civilization at the Faculty of Social Sciences and Humanities at Universiti Teknologi Malaysia (UTM). Dr. Ebrahimi has written about Iran's culture, history, religious beliefs and Malaysia's Islamic moderation, radicalism and *halal* industry from the Islamic perspective. She supervises postgraduate students and teaches various courses at undergraduate and postgraduate levels. As International Coordinator for International Academic Cooperation between South East Asia and the Middle East, she has organized international conferences on 'Issues and Challenges in The Muslim World' and 'Current Trends in the Middle East', as well as seminars and forums on the 'Israel–Palestine Conflict' with a focus on *al-Nakbah*. Her work advocates for knowledge and moderation as the truly valuable humanity module for peaceful co-existence that enriching philosophical and spiritual understanding from a pan-cultural and historical perspective. The motivation of her research field is to deliver peace and harmony focusing on the role of people's challenge in the fortune and prosperity.

Her books include *The British Role in Iranian Domestic Politics (1951–1953)* (Germany: Springer Nature, 2016); M. Ebrahimi, U. Aydemir (Eds.): *A Global Pandemic: Ripple Effects of COVID-19* (Sabah: UMS Press, 2022); M. Ebrahimi, M. Rad Goudarzi, and K. Yusoff (Eds.): *The Dynamics of Iranian Borders; Issues of Contention* (Germany: Springer Nature, 2019); M. Ebrahimi and K. Yusoff (Eds.): *The Middle East Arc of Crisis: Political Spin-off and Developmental Outcome* (Malaysia: UTM Press, 2018); M. Ebrahimi and K. Yusoff (Eds.): *The Halal Industry in Malaysia: Prospects and Challenges* (Malaysia: UTM Press, 2015); Dr. Ebrahimi has contributed to several diverse projects and published a number of journal articles, books, book chapters, and essays in academic outlets by reputable publishers. She has



S. H. bin Syed Jaafar Albar, *Ibn Khaldun's Theory and the Party-Political Edifice of the United Malays National Organisation*, SpringerBriefs in Political Science,
https://doi.org/10.1007/978-981-19-7388-8

also contributed several articles on culture, religion and history (including Malaysia, Indonesia, Middle East, Iran, Turkey and Egypt) to reputable peer-reviewed journals. Address: Mansoureh Ebrahimi, Ph.D., Faculty of Social Sciences and Humanities, Universiti Teknologi Malaysia, 81310 Johor Bahru, Johor, Malaysia.
e-mail: mansoureh@utm.my and suriebrahimi@gmail.com
Website: https://www.linkedin.com/in/suri-ebrahimi-08aa0457/;
https://publons.com/researcher/3444445/mansoureh-ebrahimi/;
http://islamic.utm.my/mansoureh/ and http://afes-press-books.de/html/APESS_29.htm.
https://orcid.org/0000-0003-2086-524X
https://scholar.google.com/citations?user=xl8ATEoAAAAJ&hl=en&oi=ao
https://www.researchgate.net/profile/Mansoureh-Ebrahimi
https://www.suriebrahimi.com/

# Glossary

## Arabic

*'asab* to bind
*'asaba* male relations in the male line
*'asabiyyah* social solidarity/group feeling
*'ilm al- 'umran* sociology or the science of being together
*'ilm al- 'umran* on social; historical development
*'ilm al- 'umran al-bashari* social development and civilisations
*'ilm al-ijtima' al-bashari* the science of human civilisation
*'ilm-al-ijtima' al-insani* the science of human society
*'imara* an edifice located in a population centre.
*'isaba / 'usba,* group
*'umr* the age of a person, a human being, a natural element.
*'umran* science of civilization/culture
*'umran* as the fact of filling an empty space.
*'umran badawi* primitive civilisation
*'umran hadhari* advanced civilisation
*'umran badaw* primitive
*'umran hadari* civilised
*'umrani* pertaining to cultural development
*Kitab al- 'Ibar* the Book of Lessons
*al- 'amr, al- 'umur, al- 'umr* life
*al-ijtima al-insani* studies on the development of society or human social organisation
*aqli* rational sciences
*badawa* Bedouins
*badawah* primitive lifestyle

© The Editor(s) (if applicable) and The Author(s), under exclusive license
to Springer Nature Singapore Pte Ltd. 2023
S. H. bin Syed Jaafar Albar, *Ibn Khaldun's Theory and the Party-Political Edifice of the United Malays National Organisation*, SpringerBriefs in Political Science,
https://doi.org/10.1007/978-981-19-7388-8

*bai'ah*   oath of loyalty
*bunyan*   an edifice or the act of building
*fiqh/Maliki fiqh*   jurisprudence
*hadara*   sedentary people
*hadarah*   advance lifestyle
*majlis al- 'ilmi*   intellectual circle
*mulk*   political power
*naqli*   acceptance of the concept that not everything can be explained by reason or
    logic but remains in the realm of divinity.
*naqli*   revealed sciences
*Ta'rif*   thirst for learning
*tafsir*   exegesis
*'umran*   a condition of being developed and flourishing town


## Malay

*adab*   good manners
*bangsa*   nation
*budibahasa*   appropriate language
*bumiputera*   son of the soil
*Bersih, Cekap dan Amanah*   Clean, Efficient and Trustworthy
*Dewan Rakyat*   Lower House of Parliament
*Hidup Melayu*   Long Live the Malays
*Kebangsaan Melayu*   Malay Nationalism
*kebangsaan*   Nationalism
*kerajaan*   a polity based on the sovereignty of a *Raja*
*Lambang Martabat Bangsa*   symbol of national dignity
*Melayu Se Malaya*   The Malay Congress of Malaya
*Mendaulatkan Martabat Bangsa*   giving sovereignty to the dignity of the Malays
**'Merdeka'**   independent or free
*'Semangat 46'*   spirit 46
*Semangat Kebangsaan*   National Spirit
*Semangat Kenegerian*   state spirit
*Bapa Pembangunan*   Father of Development
*Pengasas Kemerdekaan*   Initiator of Independence
*Pergerakan Melayu Semenanjong*   Malay Peninsula Movement
*Sejarah Penubuhan UMNO*   history of the establishment of UMNO
*Sultan-sultan kena mainkan*   The Malay Sultans had been hoodwinked
*kaum*   ethnic group
*kerajaan*   subject of the state ruler
*Kesatuan Melayu Muda*   Malay Youth Association
**Kesatuan Melayu Singapura**   Singapore Malay Union
*Ketuanan Melayu*   Malay dominance

***Kongres Melayu Se Malaya***  The Malay Congress of Malaya
***naungan***  protection/protectorate
***Parti Perikatan***  Alliance Party
***pejuang***  champion
***Pergerakan Kebangsaan Melayu***  Malay National Movement
***Perikatan***  National Alliance Organisation
***Persatuan Melayu Johor***  Johore Malay Association
**Persatuan Melayu Selangor**  Selangor Malay Association
***Persekutuan Tanah Melayu***  Federation of Malay Homelands/Federation of Malaya
***rakyat***  citizens/people
***santun***  courtesy
***semangat kenegerian***  state consciousness or loyalty to the state
***'umur***  life span of a human being

# Bibliography


Abd P (2011) The Myth of Dato' Onn Jaafar: The forgotten hero: reinventing history. Partisan Publication and Distribution, Kuala Lumpur

Abdesselem, A. Ben (1960) S.v. "Ibn Khaldun". In: Gibb HAR, Kramers JH, Levi-Provencal E and Schacht J (eds) The encyclopedia of Islam, Leiden: E.J. Brill

Adib M (2003) Reflections of free independence Malaya. Pelanduk Publications, Kuala Lumpur

Ah-Bang, Leo (1975) "New directions in Malaysia". In Southeast Asian Affairs 1975, by Institute of Southeast Asian Studies (Ed.), (87–97). Singapore: FEP International Ltd, Jurong.

Ahmad Farouk, Azeem Fazwan (2002) Culture and politics: an analysis of United Malays National Organisation (UMNO) 1946–1999. Master's Thesis. Kuala Lumpur: Universiti Malaya

Ahmad Z (2003) The epistemology of Ibn Khaldun. Routledge Curzon, London

Ahmed AS (2002) Ibn Khaldun's understanding of civilizations and the dilemmas of Islam and the west today. Middle East J 56(1):20–45

Alatas SF (2006a) Ibn Khaldun and muslim reform: toward a conceptualization. Turk J Islam Stud 16:782–795

Alatas SF (2006b) A Khaldunian exemplar for a historical sociology for the South. Curr Sociol 54(3):397–411

Alatas SF (2007) The historical sociology of Muslim societies: Khaldunian applications. Int Sociol 22(3):267–288

Alatas SF (2013) Ibn Khaldun. Oxford University Press, Oxford

Al-Ṭabbāc, Umar Fārūq (1992) Ibn Khaldūn: Fī Sīratihi Wa Falsafatihi al-Tārīkhiyyah Wa al-Ijtimāciyyah. Beirut: Mu'assasah al-Macārif

Amri L (2008) The concept of 'umran: the heuristic knot in Ibn Khaldun.J North Afr Stud 13(3):351–361 https://doi.org/10.1080/13629380701844672

Anderson B (1983) Imagined communities: reflections on the origins and spread of nationalism. Verso, London

Arnason JP, Stauth G (2004) Civilization and state formation in the Islamic context: re-reading Ibn Khaldun. Thesis Elev 76(1):29–48

Arslan A (1987) İbn-i Haldu"un İlim ve Fikir Dünyası. Ankara: Vadi Yayınları

Asad M (1961) The principles of state and government in Islam. Gibraltar: Dar Al-Andalus. Middle-East J Sci Res 11(9):1232–1237

Ashraf, Mirza Iqbal (2015) "Ibn Khaldun: The great Muslim theorist of socio-political science". https://www.academia.edu/19925990/IBN_KHALDUN_%20The_Great_Muslim_Theorist_of_Socio-Political_Science (Accessed on 3 August 2019)

Awang Z (1983) Coalition politics in Malaysia. Master's Thesis. Western Michigan University. Scholarworks@WMU. shttps://scholarworks.wmich.edu/cgi/viewcontent.cgi?article=2579&context=masters_theses

Azmeh, 'Aziz (2003) Ibn Khaldūn: an essay in reinterpretation. Central European University Press, Budapest

Baali F (1988) Society, state, and urbanism: Ibn Khaldun's sociological thought. University of New York Press, New York

Brown G (2008) Federal and state elections in Malaysia, March 2008. Elect Stud 27(4):740–744

Brown, Rewcastle Clare (2018) The sarawak report: the inside story of the 1MDB exposé. Lost World Press. Petaling Jaya: Gerakbudaya Enterprise

Caksu A (2007) Ibn Khaldun and Hegel on causality in history: Aristotelian legacy reconsidered. Asian J Soc Sci 35(1):47–83

Calvert, John CM (1984) "Ibn Khaldun and the orientalist historiography of the Maghrib". Master's Thesis. McGill University. https://dokumen.tips/documents/ibn-khaldun-and-the-orientalist-historiography-of-i-ibn-khaldun-and-the.html?page=1

Campo, Juan E (2009) "Ibn Khaldun, Abd al-Rahman ibn Muhammad". In: Juan E (ed) The encyclopedia of Islam, Campo, New York: Facts of File

Case W (2010) Malaysia's 2008 general election—transition from single-party dominance? J Curr Southeast Asian Aff 29(2):121–156

Chin J, Huat WC (2009) Malaysia's electoral upheaval. J Democr 20(3):71–85

Cheah Boon Kheng (1979) The Malayan democratic union 1945–1948. Master's Thesis. Kuala Lumpur: Universiti Malaya

Cheah Boon Kheng (1988) The erosion of ideological hegemony and royal power and the rise of postwar Malay nationalism 1945–46. J Southeast Asian Stud 19(1):1–26

Cheah Boon Kheng (2007) New perspectives & research on Malaysian history. Malaysian Branch of the Royal Asiatic Society, Kuala Lumpur

Cheddadi, Abdesselam (2005) "Recognising the importance of Ibn Khaldun". Interview, 11 November. France Diplomacy. https://www.diplomatie.gouv.fr/IMG/pdf/Cheddadieng.pdf

Cowan JM (1974) A dictionary of modern written Arabic (Arabic-English). Macdonald and Evans Ltd., London

Datar KK (1983) Quest for politics of consensus. New Delhi: Vikos

Dhaouadi M (2005) The Ibar: lessons of Ibn Khaldun's Umran Mind. Contemp Sociol 34(6):585–591. https://doi.org/10.1177/009430610503400602

Dhaouadi M (1990) Ibn Khaldun: the founding father of eastern sociology. Int Sociol 5(3):319–335. https://doi.org/10.1177/026858090005003007

Durkheim E (1997) The division of labor in society. The Free Press, New York

Edwards, Scott (2018) Reports: Malaysia's elections: corruption, foreign money, and burying-the hatchet politics. 10 June. Al Jazeera Centre for Studies. https://studies.aljazeera.net/en/reports/2018/06/malaysias-elections-corruption-foreign-money-burying-hatchet-politics-180610090147666.html

El-Rayes, Waseem (2008) The political aspects of Ibn Khaldun's study of culture and history. PhD Dissertation. United States, College Park: University of Maryland,

Enan, Mohammad Abdullah (1979) Ibn Khaldun: his life and works. New Delhi: Kitab Bhavan

Esteban, Damian (2004) Religion and the state in Ibn Khaldun's Muqaddimah. Master's Thesis. McGill University. McGill University's digital repository. https://escholarship.mcgill.ca/concern/theses/8910jv21p

Faaland, Just Parkinson JR, Saniman, Rais (1990) Growth and ethnic inequality. Malaysi's new economic policy. Kuala Lumpur: Dewan Bahasa dan Pustaka

Fischel, Walter (1967) Ibn Khaldun in Egypt: his publications and his historical research (1382–1406). A Study in Islamic Historiography. Berkeley and Los Angeles. University of California Press

Fromherz AJ (2011) Ibn Khaldun: life and times. Edinburgh University Press, Edinburgh

Funston J (1980) Malay politics in Malaysia: a study of the United Malays, National Organisation and Parti Islam. Kuala Lumpur: Heinemann Asia

Funston J (2018) Malaysia's 14th general election (GE14)—The contest for the Malay electorate. J Curr Southeast Asian Aff. 37(3):57–83. https://doi.org/10.1177/186810341803700304

Friedman G (2018) The role of political leaders. Geopolitical future. https://geopoliticalfutures.com/role-political-leaders/

Garrison DH (2012) Ibn Khaldun and the modern social sciences: a comparative theoretical inquiry into society, the state, and revolution. Master's Thesis. University of Denver. https://digitalcommons.du.edu/etd/231

Gellner E (1982) Reviewed work: "Ibn Khaldun and Islamic thought-styles: a social perspective" by Baali, Fuad & Wardi. Ali. Br J Sociol 33(2):295–296. https://doi.org/10.2307/589949

Ghazali, Abdullah Zakaria (2012) Persekutuan Tanah Melayu Merdeka, 31 Ogos 1957: Liku dan Jejak Perjuangan Patriot dan Nasionalis Menentang British. Persatuan Sejarah Malaysia Repositori Digital@PNM. https://myrepositori.pnm.gov.my/bitstream/123456789/3625/1/MDSS_2012_40_01.pdf

Gibb HAR (1933) The Islamic background of Ibn Khaldun's political theory. Bull Sch Orient Stud 7(1):23–31

Gomez ET, Kaur S (2014) Struggling for power: policies, coalition politics and elections in Malaysia. University of Malaya, Kuala Lumpur

Goodman LE (1972) Ibn Khaldun and Thucydides. J Am Orient Soc 92(2):250–270

Gunasegaram P, Kinibiz (2018) 1MDB: The scandal that brought down a government. Strategic Information and Research Development Centre, Malaysia

Gungwu, Wang (1981) Malayan nationalism. community and nation: Essays on Southeast Asia and the Chinese. Kuala Lumpur: Heinemann Educational Books.

Halim, Asyiqin A (2012) The application of Ibn Khaldūn's theory of Asabiyyah to the modern period with special reference to the Malay Muslim community in Malaysia. PhD Thesis. University of Birmingham

Hodgson MGS (2009) The venture of Islam, volume 1: the classical age of Islam. Chicago: University of Chicago Press

Hodgson MGS (1974) The venture of Islam: conscience and history in a world civilization. University of Chicago, Chicago

Hutchinson FE, Lee HA (eds) (2019) The defeat of barisan nasional: Missed Signs or Late Surge? ISEAS Publishing, Singapore

Ibn Khaldun (1974) in Dawood NJ (Ed.), The Muqaddimah (The Introduction), Princeton University Press, Princeton, NJ, (translated by Franz Rosenthal)

Khaldun I (1958) The Muqaddimah: an introduction to history. (trans: Rosenthal F), 1st edn. Princeton University Press, New York

Khaldun I (1967) The Muqaddimah· An Introduction to History. (trans: Rosenthal F) abridged and NJ Dawood NJ (ed), 2nd edn. Routledge & Kegan Paul Ltd. and Martin Secker and Warburg Ltd., London

Khaldun I (2005) *The Muqaddimah: An Introduction to History.* Translated by F. Rosenthal; abridged and edited by N. J. Dawood; with a new introduction by B. Lawrence, 3rd edn. Princeton University Press, Bollingen Series, Princeton and Oxford

Ibn Khaldun (2017) Ibn Khaldun on sufism: rRemedy for the question in search of answers. (trans: Ozer Y). Cambridge: The Islamic Texts Society.

Ibn Khaldun (2020) *Mukaddime: Ibn Haldun.* (trans: Uludağ S). Istanbul: Dergah Yayinlari

Imam SMA (1978) Some aspects of Ibn-Khaldun's socio-political analysis of history: a critical appreciation. Karachi: Khurasan Islamic Research Centre.

Irwin R (2018) Ibn Khaldun: an intellectual biography. Princeton University Press, New Jersey

Jason Wei JN, Rangel JG, Yet CP (2021) Malaysia's 14th General Election: dissecting the 'Malaysian tsunami'—measuring the impacts of ethnicity and urban development on electoral outcomes. Asian J Polit Sci 29(1):42–66. https://doi.org/10.1080/02185377.2020.1814363

Jaymal SZ (2008) UMNO's Keris is here to stay. Malaysiakini, 6 November. Available online at: http://www.malaysiakini.com/news/74414

Kassim, Shahidan (2006) UMNO: Satu Kajian Kelangsungan Parti Politik Melayu. PhD. Thesis. Universiti Utara Malaysia. http://etd.uum.edu.my/3655/

Kayapınar, M. Akif (2006) "İbn Haldûn'un Asabiyet Kavramı: Siyaset Teorisinde Yeni Bir Açılım (Ibn Khaldun's Concept of Asabiyyah: a new expansion in political theory)". Turk J Islam Stud. (15): 83–114. https://dergipark.org.tr/en/pub/isad/issue/68676/1078999

Kayapınar MA (2008) Ibn Khaldun's concept of Asabiyyah: an alternative tool for understanding long-term politics? Asian J Soc Sci 36(3–4):375–407. https://doi.org/10.1163/156853108X32 7010

Kee Thuan Chye (Ed) (2008) March 8: The day Malaysia woke up. Subang, Malaysia: Marshall Cavendish

Kessler Clive (2018) "Malaysia's electoral fantasy belies worrying reality". 29 April. East Asia Forum. https://www.eastasiaforum.org/2018/04/29/malaysias-electoral-fantasy-bel ies-worrying-reality/

Khoon TC (1985) Malaysia today. Pelanduk Publications, Kuala Lumpur

Lacoste Y (1984) Ibn Khaldun: The birth of history and the past of the third world. Verso, London

Lane EW (1968) An Arabic-English Lexicon. Volume Two. Lebanon: Librairie Du Liban

Lawrence BB (1983) Introduction: Ibn Khaldun and Islamic ideology. J Asian Afr Stud 18(3–4):154–165

Lee HG, Nesadurai HES (2010) "Political transition in Malaysia: the future of Malaysia's hybrid political regime". In: Mely Caballero-Anthony (ed) Political change, democratic transition and security in Southeast Asia, London and New York: Routledge, pp 97–123

Leetee, Richard (2007) From Kampung to twin towers. Kuala Lumpur: Oxford Fajar

Mahdi M (1957) Ibn Khaldun's philosophy of history: a study in the philosophic foundation of the science of culture. G. Allen and Unwin, London

*Malaysiakini* (2018) Call me racist but Malays are in decline and it's our fault—Dr M. 29 December. https://www.malaysiakini.com/news/458169

Malaysia Parliamentary Chamber: Dewan Rakyat, Election Held in 1999. Available online at: http://archive.ipu.org/parline-e/reports/arc/2197_99.htm

Mauzy, Diane K (1982) Barisan nasional: coalition government in Malaysia. Kuala Lumpur: Marican

Mohamad M (2008) Malaysia: democracy and the end of ethnic politics? Aust J Int Aff 62(4):441–459

McKie RCH (1963) The emergence of Malaysia. Greenwood Press, Connecticut

Miller H (1965) The story of Malaysia. Faber & Faber, London

Mohd Basri, Ahmad Fawzi (1992) The United Malays National Organization (UMNO) 1981–1991: a study of the mechanics of a changing political culture. PhD Thesis. University of Hull

Moniruzzaman M, Farzana KF (2018) Malaysia' 14th general election: end of an epoch, and beginning of a new? Intellect Discourse 26(1):207–228

Monteil, Vincent (1967) Discours sur l'histoire universelle (Al-Muqaddima)—Traduction nouvelle, préf. et notes par Vincent Monteil. Beirut: Commission internationale pour la traduction des chefs-d'oeuvre.

Moten AR (2006) The 2004 general elections in Malaysia: a mandate to rule. Asian Surv 46(2):319–340

Nordlinger EA (1972) Conflict regulation in divided societies. Harvard University Press, Cambridge, Massachusetts

Omar A (1999) *"Malaya/Malaysia: state, nation, nationality, the emergence of nationhood in a vacuum"*. Paper presented at a conference on "concepts of state, identity and nationhood in Southeast Asia", at the National University of Singapore, Kent Ridge, Singapore, 8–11 December 1999

Ong Kian Ming (2008) "Making sense of the political tsunami". Malaysiakini. 11 March. http://www.malaysiakini.com/news/79604.com

Ong Kian Ming (2018) GE14—A truly Malaysian Tsunami. Available online at: https://dapmal aysia.org/statements/2018/05/17/27122/

Ooi Kee Beng, Johan Saravanamuttu, Lee Hock Guan (2008) March 8: Eclipsing May 13. Singapore: Institute of Southeast Asian Studies

Osman AS (2004) Hubungan antara Asabiyyah dan keruntuhan Kerajaan Baniumayyah: suatu analisis menurut Ibn Khaldun. Jurnal Intelek 2(1):54–61

Osmani NM, Nurullah AS (2009) "Ibn Khaldun's Muqaddimah and 'Ilm Al-'Umran: an analysis". In: Bakar O, Ahmad B (eds) Proceedings of Ibn Khaldun's legacy and its significance, Kuala Lumpur: International Institute of Islamic Thought and Civilization ISTAC, pp 89–102

Ozey, Mehmet (1988) Development in Malaysia: poverty, wealth and trusteeship. Kuala Lumpur: INSAN

Panebianco A (1988) Political parties: organization and power. Cambridge University Press, Cambridge

Pepinsky TB (2009) The 2008 Malaysian elections: an end to ethnic politics? J East Asian Stud 9(1):87–120

Purcell V (1948) The Chinese in Malaya. Oxford University Press, London

Ra'ees, Wahabuddin (2004) Asabiyyah, religion and regime types: re-reading Ibn Khaldun. Intellect Discourse 12(2):159–180

Ra'ees, Wahabuddin (2013) "Building Islamic polity within a secular framework of political activity in Egypt, Tunisia and Turkey with reference to Ibn Khaldun's Theory of State". Al-Shajarah: J Int Inst Islam Thought Civlzation, 18(1): 59–84

Rahman, Serina (2018) "When Malaysian youth take a stand… a wave of change follows". 14 May, ISEAS-Yusuf Ishak's. https://www.iseas.edu.sg/media/commentaries/when-malaysian-youth-take-a-stand-a-wave-of-change-follows-by-serina-rahman/

Roff WR (1967) The oOrigins of Malay nationalism. Yale University Press, USA

Roslan AH (2001) Income inequality, poverty and development policy in Malaysia. Universiti Utara Malaysia, Kedah: School of Economics. https://www.semanticscholar.org/paper/Inc ome-Inequality-%2C-Poverty-and-Development-Policy-Roslan/b93d23e72af6e595f5496483 15f7234ea3bba61c

Sidani Y (2008) Ibn Khaldun of North Africa: An AD 1377 theory of leadership. J Manag Hist 14(1):73–86

Schleifer A (1985) Ibn Khaldun's theories of perception, logic & knowledge: an Islamic phenomenology. Am J Islam Soc Sci 2:225–231

Schmidt N (1978) Ibn Khaldun: historian, sociologist and philosopher. Universal Books, Lahore

Silcock TH (1949) Forces for unity in Malaya: observations of a European Resident. Int Aff 25(4):453–465. https://doi.org/10.2307/3018421

Simon, Robert (2002) Ibn Khaldun: history as science and the patrimonial empire. Budapest: Akadémiai Kiadó

Stockwell AJ (1979) British policy and Malay politics during the Malayan union experiment 1945–1948. Kuala Lumpur: MBRAS

Sopiee MN (2005) From Malayan Union to Singapore separation: political unification in the Malaysia region, 1945–1965. University Malaya Press, Kuala Lumpur, Malaysia

Sümer B (2012) Ibn Khaldun's Asabiyyah for social cohesion. Electron J Soc Sci 11(41):253–267

Sultan Nazrin Shah (2008) "Regent of Perak Raja Nazrin Shah's address at the Conference of Malaysian Judges". 9 April. The Malaysian Bar. https://www.malaysianbar.org.my/article/ news/speeches/speeches/regent-of-perak-raja-nazrin-shah-s-address-at-the-conference-of-mal aysian-judges (accessed on 3 August 2022).

Teik KB (2010) Commentary The Malaysian general election of 29 November 1999. Aust J Polit Sci 35(2):305–311. https://doi.org/10.1080/713649324

Thorbecke E, Charumilind C (2002) Economic inequality and its socioeconomic impact. World Dev 30(9):1477–1495

Tibi B (1997) Arab nationalism—Between Islam and the Nation-State. Macmillan Press Ltd., London

*Today* (2018) Once dominant, Malaysia's BN records lowest-ever vote share of 36.4% in 2018 GE. 11 May. https://www.todayonline.com/malaysian-ge/3642-cent-bn-records-lowest-popular-vote-history (Accessed on 3 August 2019)

Tong, Liew Chin (2019). "Premature to do GE15 storyboard". New Straits Times. 29 July. https://www.nst.com.my/opinion/columnists/2019/07/508106/premature-do-ge15-storyboard (Accessed on 4 August 2022)

Ufen A (2008) The 2008 elections in Malaysia: uncertainties of electoral authoritarianism. Taiwan J Democr 4(1):155–169

UMNO Information. (n.d.). UMNO History. Retrieved from UMNO Malaysia: https://umno.org.my/en/sejarah/

UMNO Johor. (n.d). Sejarah UMNO Johor. https://umnojohorofficial.wordpress.com/berita-terkini/ w

Wahid A, Abidin Z (1977) Semangat Perjuangan Melayu. Jebat: Malaysian. J Hist, Polit Strat Stud 07–08:1–9

Wan Ahmed, Sharifah Sofia (2010) Culture, power and resistance: post-colonialism, autobiography and Malaysian Independence. PhD Thesis. School of Applied Social Sciences, Durham University

Wan Razali, Wan Mohd Fazrul (2014) Al-Ashariyyah Menurut Ibn Khaldun: Sejarawan Dan Ahli Sosiologi Islam. PhD Thesis. Bangi, Selangor: Universiti Kebangsaan Malaysia

Wan Teh, Wan Hashim (2017) "Fasa Pertama Perjuangan UMNO Penuh Berani". Utusan Malaysia (UM). 11 May. https://wajabangsa.blogspot.com/2017/05/fasa-pertama-perjuangan-umno-penuh.html (accessed on 1 August 2022).

Welsh, Bridget (2008) "Election Post-Mortem: Top 10 Factors". Malaysiakini. 12 March. http://www.malaysiakini.com/news/79677.com

Welsh B (ed) (2018a) The end of UMNO?: essays on Malaysia's dominant party. Strategic Information and Research Development Centre (SIRD), Malaysia

Welsh B (2018b) "Saviour" politics and Malaysia's 2018 electoral democratic breakthrough: rethinking explanatory narratives and implications. J Curr Southeast Asian Aff. 37(3):85–108. https://doi.org/10.1177/186810341803700305

White A (2009) An Islamic approach to studying history: reflections on Ibn Khaldun's deterministic historical approach. Intellect Discourse 17(2):221–244

Winstedt R (1948) Malaya and its history. Hutchinson's University Library, London

Wright T, Hope B (2018) Billion dollar whale: the man who fooled wall street, hollywood, and the world. Hachette Books, New York